FOREWORD

The collection of "Everything Will Be Okay" travel phrasebooks published by T&P Books is designed for people traveling abroad for tourism and business. The phrasebooks contain what matters most - the essentials for basic communication. This is an indispensable set of phrases to "survive" while abroad.

This phrasebook will help you in most cases where you need to ask something, get directions, find out how much something costs, etc. It can also resolve difficult communication situations where gestures just won't help.

This book contains a lot of phrases that have been grouped according to the most relevant topics. A separate section of the book also provides a small dictionary with more than 1,500 important and useful words.

Take "Everything Will Be Okay" phrasebook with you on the road and you'll have an irreplaceable traveling companion who will help you find your way out of any situation and teach you to not fear speaking with foreigners.

TABLE OF CONTENTS

T&P Books Publishing

T&P Books Publishing

PHRASEBOOK

BELARUSIAN

THE MOST IMPORTANT PHRASES

This phrasebook contains
the most important
phrases and questions
for basic communication
Everything you need
to survive overseas

T&P BOOKS

By Andrey Taranov

Phrasebook + 1500-word dictionary

English-Belarusian phrasebook & concise dictionary

By Andrey Taranov

The collection of "Everything Will Be Okay" travel phrasebooks published by T&P Books is designed for people traveling abroad for tourism and business. The phrasebooks contain what matters most - the essentials for basic communication. This is an indispensable set of phrases to "survive" while abroad.

Another section of the book also provides a small dictionary with more than 1,500 useful words arranged alphabetically. The dictionary includes a lot of gastronomic terms and will be helpful when ordering food at a restaurant or buying groceries at the store.

T&P Books Publishing
www.tpbooks.com

ISBN: 978-1-78616-753-8

This book is also available in E-book formats.
Please visit www.tpbooks.com or the major online bookstores.

PRONUNCIATION

Letter	Belarusian example	T&P phonetic alphabet	English example
A a	Англія	[a]	shorter than in ask
Б б	бульба	[b]	baby, book
В в	вечар	[v]	very, river
Г г	галава	[ɦ]	between [g] and [h]
Д д	дзіця	[d]	day, doctor
Дж дж	джаз	[ʤ]	joke, general
Е е	метр	[ɛ]	man, bad
Ё ё	вясёлы	[jɔ]	New York
Ж ж	жыццё	[ʒ]	forge, pleasure
З з	заўтра	[z]	zebra, please
I i	нізкі	[i]	shorter than in feet
Й й	англійскі	[j]	yes, New York
К к	красавік	[k]	clock, kiss
Л л	лінія	[l]	lace, people
М м	камень	[m]	magic, milk
Н н	Новы год	[n]	name, normal
О о	опера	[ɔ]	bottle, doctor
П п	піва	[p]	pencil, private
Р р	морква	[r]	rice, radio
С с	соль	[s]	city, boss
Т т	трус	[t]	tourist, trip
У у	ізумруд	[u]	book
Ў ў	каўбаса	[w]	vase, winter
Ф ф	футра	[f]	face, food
Х х	захад	[h]	home, have
Ц ц	цэнтр	[ts]	cats, tsetse fly
Ч ч	пачатак	[ʧ], [ɕ]	church, French
Ш ш	штодня	[ʃ]	machine, shark
Ь ь	попельніца	[ʲ]	soft sign - no sound
Ы ы	рыжы	[ɨ]	big, America
'	сузор'е	[ˀ]	hard sign, no sound
Э э	Грэцыя	[ɛ]	man, bad
Ю ю	плюс	[ʉ]	youth, usually
Я я	трусяня	[ja], [ˈa]	royal

Letter	Belarusian example	T&P phonetic alphabet	English example

Combinations of letters

дз	дзень	[ʣ]	beads, kids
дзь	лебедзь	[ʣ]	jeans, gene
дж	джаз	[ʤ]	joke, general

LIST OF ABBREVIATIONS

English abbreviations

ab.	-	about
adj	-	adjective
adv	-	adverb
anim.	-	animate
as adj	-	attributive noun used as adjective
e.g.	-	for example
etc.	-	et cetera
fam.	-	familiar
fem.	-	feminine
form.	-	formal
inanim.	-	inanimate
masc.	-	masculine
math	-	mathematics
mil.	-	military
n	-	noun
pl	-	plural
pron.	-	pronoun
sb	-	somebody
sing.	-	singular
sth	-	something
v aux	-	auxiliary verb
vi	-	intransitive verb
vi, vt	-	intransitive, transitive verb
vt	-	transitive verb

Belarusian abbreviations

ж	-	feminine noun
ж мн	-	feminine plural
м	-	masculine noun
м мн	-	masculine plural
м, ж	-	masculine, feminine
мн	-	plural
н	-	neuter
н мн	-	neuter plural

BELARUSIAN PHRASEBOOK

This section contains
important phrases that may
come in handy in various
real-life situations.
The phrasebook will help
you ask for directions, clarify
a price, buy tickets, and
order food at a restaurant

T&P Books Publishing

PHRASEBOOK CONTENTS

T&P Books Publishing

The bare minimum

Excuse me, …	**Прабачце, …** [pra'batʃtse, …]
Hello.	**Прывітанне.** [privi'tanne.]
Thank you.	**Дзякуй.** [dzʲakuj.]
Good bye.	**Да пабачэння.** [da paba'tʃɛnnʲa.]
Yes.	**Так.** [tak.]
No.	**Не.** [ne.]
I don't know.	**Я ня ведаю.** [ʲa nʲa 'vedau.]
Where? | Where to? | When?	**Дзе? | Куды? | Калі?** [dze? | ku'dɨ? | ka'li?]
I need …	**Мне трэба …** [mne 'trɛba …]
I want …	**Я хачу …** [ʲa ha'tʃu …]
Do you have …?	**У вас ёсць …?** [u vas ʲostsʲ …?]
Is there a … here?	**Тут ёсць …?** [tut ʲostsʲ …?]
May I …?	**Я магу …?** [ʲa ma'ɦu …?]
…, please (polite request)	**Калі ласка** [ka'li 'laska]
I'm looking for …	**Я шукаю …** [ʲa ʃu'kau …]
restroom	**туалет** [tua'let]
ATM	**банкамат** [banka'mat]
pharmacy (drugstore)	**аптэку** [ap'tɛku]
hospital	**бальніцу** [balj'nitsu]
police station	**аддзяленне міліцыі** [adzʲa'lenne mi'litsii]
subway	**метро** [me'trɔ]

taxi	таксі [tak'si]
train station	вакзал [vak'zal]

My name is ...	Мяне завуць ... [mʲa'ne za'vutsʲ ...]
What's your name?	Як вас завуць? [ʲak vas za'vutsʲ?]
Could you please help me?	Дапамажыце мне, калі ласка. [dapama'ʒɨtse mne, ka'li 'laska?]
I've got a problem.	У мяне праблема. [u mʲa'ne prab'lema.]
I don't feel well.	Мне дрэнна. [mne 'drɛnna.]
Call an ambulance!	Выклікайце хуткую дапамогу! [vɨklikajtse 'hutkuʉ dapa'mɔɦu!]
May I make a call?	Магу я пазваніць? [ma'ɦu ʲa pazva'nitsʲ?]

I'm sorry.	Выбачце. [vibatʃtse.]
You're welcome.	Калі ласка. [ka'li 'laska.]

I, me	я [ʲa]
you (inform.)	ты [tɨ]
he	ён [ʲon]
she	яна [ʲa'na]
they (masc.)	яны [ʲa'nɨ]
they (fem.)	яны [ʲa'ni]
we	мы [mɨ]
you (pl)	вы [vɨ]
you (sg, form.)	вы [vɨ]

ENTRANCE	УВАХОД [uva'hɔd]
EXIT	ВЫХАД [vihad]
OUT OF ORDER	НЕ ПРАЦУЕ [ne pra'tsue]
CLOSED	ЗАЧЫНЕНА [za'tʃinena]

OPEN | **АДЧЫНЕНА**
[at'ʧinena]

FOR WOMEN | **ДЛЯ ЖАНЧЫН**
[dlʲa ʒan'ʧin]

FOR MEN | **ДЛЯ МУЖЧЫН**
[dlʲa muʒ'ʧin]

Questions

Where?	**Дзе?** [dze?]
Where to?	**Куды?** [ku'dɨ?]
Where from?	**Адкуль?** [at'kulʲ?]
Why?	**Чаму?** [tʃa'mu?]
For what reason?	**Навошта?** [na'vɔʃta?]
When?	**Калі?** [ka'li?]

How long?	**Як доўга?** [ʲak 'dowha?]
At what time?	**У колькі ?** [u 'kɔlʲki?]
How much?	**Колькі каштуе?** [kɔlʲki kaʃ'tue?]
Do you have ...?	**У вас ёсць ...?** [u vas ʲostsʲ ...?]
Where is ...?	**Дзе знаходзіцца ...?** [dze zna'hɔdzitsa ...?]

What time is it?	**Колькі часу?** [kɔlʲki 'tʃasu?]
May I make a call?	**Магу я пазваніць?** [ma'hu ʲa pazva'nitsʲ?]
Who's there?	**Хто там?** [htɔ tam?]
Can I smoke here?	**Тут дазволена курыць?** [tut daz'vɔlena ku'rɨtsʲ?]
May I ...?	**Я магу ...?** [ʲa ma'hu ...?]

Needs

I'd like …	**Я б хацеў /хацела/ …** [ˈa b haˈtsew /haˈtsela/ …]
I don't want …	**Я не хачу …** [ˈa ne haˈtʃu …]
I'm thirsty.	**Я хачу піць.** [ˈa haˈtʃu pitsʲ.]
I want to sleep.	**Я хачу спаць.** [ˈa haˈtʃu spatsʲ.]
I want …	**Я хачу …** [ˈa haˈtʃu …]
to wash up	**памыцца** [paˈmitsa]
to brush my teeth	**пачысціць зубы** [paˈtʃisʲtsitsʲ ˈzubi]
to rest a while	**крыху адпачыць** [krihu adpaˈtʃitsʲ]
to change my clothes	**пераапрануцца** [peraapraˈnutsa]
to go back to the hotel	**вярнуцца ў гасцініцу** [vʲarˈnutsa w hasʲˈtsinitsu]
to buy …	**купіць …** [kuˈpitsʲ …]
to go to …	**з'ездзіць у …** [zˈezdzitsʲ u …]
to visit …	**наведаць …** [naˈvedatsʲ …]
to meet with …	**сустрэцца з …** [susˈtrɛtsa z …]
to make a call	**пазваніць** [pazvaˈnitsʲ]
I'm tired.	**Я стаміўся /стамілася/.** [ˈa staˈmiwsʲa /staˈmilasʲa/.]
We are tired.	**Мы стаміліся.** [mi staˈmilisʲa.]
I'm cold.	**Мне холадна.** [mne ˈholadna.]
I'm hot.	**Мне горача.** [mne ˈhoratʃa.]
I'm OK.	**Мне нармальна.** [mne narˈmalʲna.]

I need to make a call.

Мне трэба пазваніць.
[mne 'trɛba pazva'nitsʲ.]

I need to go to the restroom.

Мне трэба ў туалет.
[mne 'trɛba w tua'let.]

I have to go.

Мне трэба ісці.
[mne 'trɛba isʲtsi.]

I have to go now.

Мне трэба ісці.
[mne 'trɛba isʲtsi.]

Asking for directions

Excuse me, …	**Прабачце, …** [pra'batʃtse, …]
Where is …?	**Дзе знаходзіцца …?** [dze zna'hodzitsa …?]
Which way is …?	**У якім напрамку знаходіцца …?** [u ʲa'kim na'pramku zna'hoditsa …?]
Could you help me, please?	**Дапамажыце мне, калі ласка.** [dapama'ʒitse mne, ka'li 'laska.]
I'm looking for …	**Я шукаю …** [ʲa ʃu'kaʉ …]
I'm looking for the exit.	**Я шукаю выхад.** [ʲa ʃu'kaʉ 'vihad.]
I'm going to …	**Я еду ў …** [ʲa 'edu w …]
Am I going the right way to …?	**Ці правільна я іду …?** [tsi 'praviĺna ʲa idu …?]
Is it far?	**Гэта далёка?** [hɛta da'lʲoka?]
Can I get there on foot?	**Я дайду туды пешшу?** [ʲa daj'du tu'di 'peʃu?]
Can you show me on the map?	**Пакажыце мне на карце, калі ласка.** [paka'ʒitse mne na kartse, ka'li 'laska.]
Show me where we are right now.	**Пакажыце, дзе мы зараз.** [paka'ʒitse, dze mi 'zaraz.]
Here	**Тут** [tut]
There	**Там** [tam]
This way	**Сюды** [sʉ'di]
Turn right.	**Павярніце направа.** [pavʲar'nitse na'prava.]
Turn left.	**Павярніце налева** [pavʲar'nitse na'leva.]
first (second, third) turn	**першы (другі, трэці) паварот** [perʃi (dru'hi, 'trɛtsi) pava'rot]
to the right	**направа** [na'prava]

to the left

налева
[na'leva]

Go straight ahead.

Ідзіце прама.
[i'dzitse 'prama.]

Signs

WELCOME!	**САРДЭЧНА ЗАПРАШАЕМ!** [sar'dɛtʃna zapra'ʃaem!]
ENTRANCE	**УВАХОД** [uva'hɔd]
EXIT	**ВЫХАД** [vɨhad]
PUSH	**АД СЯБЕ** [at sʲa'be]
PULL	**НА СЯБЕ** [na sʲa'be]
OPEN	**АДЧЫНЕНА** [at'tʃɨnena]
CLOSED	**ЗАЧЫНЕНА** [za'tʃɨnena]
FOR WOMEN	**ДЛЯ ЖАНЧЫН** [dlʲa ʒan'tʃɨn]
FOR MEN	**ДЛЯ МУЖЧЫН** [dlʲa muʒ'tʃɨn]
GENTLEMEN, GENTS (m)	**МУЖЧЫНСКІ ТУАЛЕТ** [muʒ'tʃɨnski tua'let]
WOMEN (f)	**ЖАНОЧЫ ТУАЛЕТ** [ʒa'nɔtʃi tua'let]
DISCOUNTS	**ЗНІЖКІ** [zniʒki]
SALE	**РАСПРОДАЖ** [ras'prɔdaʃ]
FREE	**БЯСПЛАТНА** [bʲas'platna]
NEW!	**НАВІНКА!** [na'vinka!]
ATTENTION!	**УВАГА!** [u'vaɦa!]
NO VACANCIES	**МЕСЦАЎ НЯМА** [mesʲtsaw nʲa'ma]
RESERVED	**ЗАРЭЗЕРВАВАНА** [zarɛzerva'vana]
ADMINISTRATION	**АДМІНІСТРАЦЫЯ** [admini'stratsʲɨa]
STAFF ONLY	**ТОЛЬКІ ДЛЯ ПЕРСАНАЛУ** [tɔlʲki dlʲa persa'nalu]

BEWARE OF THE DOG!	**ЗЛЫ САБАКА** [zlɨ sa'baka]
NO SMOKING!	**НЕ КУРЫЦЬ!** [ne ku'ritsʲ!]
DO NOT TOUCH!	**РУКАМІ НЕ КРАНАЦЬ!** [ru'kami ne kra'natsʲ!]
DANGEROUS	**НЕБЯСПЕЧНА** [nebʲa'spetʃna]
DANGER	**НЕБЯСПЕКА** [nebʲa'speka]
HIGH VOLTAGE	**ВЫСОКАЕ НАПРУЖАННЕ** [vɨ'sɔkae nap'ruʒanne]
NO SWIMMING!	**КУПАЦЦА ЗАБАРОНЕНА** [ku'patsa zaba'rɔnena]
OUT OF ORDER	**НЕ ПРАЦУЕ** [ne pra'tsue]
FLAMMABLE	**ВОГНЕНЕБЯСПЕЧНА** [vɔɦnenebʲas'petʃna]
FORBIDDEN	**ЗАБАРОНЕНА** [zaba'rɔnena]
NO TRESPASSING!	**ПРАХОД ЗАБАРОНЕНЫ** [pra'hɔd zaba'rɔnenɨ]
WET PAINT	**АФАРБАВАНА** [afarba'vana]
CLOSED FOR RENOVATIONS	**ЗАЧЫНЕНА НА РАМОНТ** [za'tʃɨnena na ra'mɔnt]
WORKS AHEAD	**РАМОНТНЫЯ РАБОТЫ** [ra'mɔntnɨʲa ra'botɨ]
DETOUR	**АБ'ЕЗД** [a'bʲezt]

Transportation. General phrases

| plane | самалёт
[sama'lʲot] |
| train | цягнік
[tsʲah'nik] |
| bus | аўтобус
[aw'tɔbus] |
| ferry | паром
[pa'rɔm] |
| taxi | таксі
[tak'si] |
| car | машына
[ma'ʃɨna] |

| schedule | расклад руху
[ras'klad 'ruhu] |
| Where can I see the schedule? | Дзе можна паглядзець расклад руху?
[dze 'mɔʒna paɦlʲa'dzetsʲ ras'klad 'ruhu?] |

| workdays (weekdays) | працоўныя дні
[pra'tsɔwnʲʲa dni] |
| weekends | выхадныя дні
[vɨhad'nʲʲa dni] |
| holidays | святочныя дні
[svʲa'tɔtʃnʲʲa dni] |

| DEPARTURE | АДПРАЎЛЕННЕ
[adpraw'lenne] |
| ARRIVAL | ПРЫБЫЦЦЁ
[prɨbɨ'tsʲo] |
| DELAYED | ЗАТРЫМЛІВАЕЦЦА
[za'trimlivaetsa] |
| CANCELLED | АДМЕНЕНЫ
[ad'meneni] |

| next (train, etc.) | наступны
[na'stupni] |
| first | першы
[perʃi] |
| last | апошні
[a'pɔʃni] |

When is the next ...?	**Калі будзе наступны ...?** [ka'li 'budze na'stupnі ...?]
When is the first ...?	**Калі адыходзіць першы ...?** [ka'li adіhɔdzіtsʲ 'perʃі ...?]
When is the last ...?	**Калі адыходзіць апошні ...?** [ka'li adіhɔdzіtsʲ a'pɔʃnі ...?]

transfer (change of trains, etc.)	**перасадка** [pera'satka]
to make a transfer	**зрабіць перасадку** [zra'bitsʲ pera'satku]
Do I need to make a transfer?	**Мне патрэбна рабіць перасадку?** [mne pa'trɛbna ra'bitsʲ pera'satku?]

Buying tickets

Where can I buy tickets?	**Дзе я магу купіць білеты?** [dze ʲa maˈɦu kuˈpitsʲ biˈleti?]
ticket	**білет** [biˈlet]
to buy a ticket	**купіць білет** [kuˈpitsʲ biˈlet]
ticket price	**кошт білета** [kɔʃt biˈleta]
Where to?	**Куды?** [kuˈdɨ?]
To what station?	**Да якой станцыі?** [da ʲaˈkɔj ˈstantsɨi?]
I need …	**Мне трэба …** [mne ˈtrɛba …]
one ticket	**адзін білет** [aˈdzin biˈlet]
two tickets	**два білета** [dva biˈleta]
three tickets	**тры білета** [tri biˈleta]
one-way	**у адзін бок** [u aˈdzin bɔk]
round-trip	**туды і назад** [tuˈdɨ i naˈzad]
first class	**першы клас** [perʃi klas]
second class	**другі клас** [druˈɦi klas]
today	**сёння** [sʲonnʲa]
tomorrow	**заўтра** [zawtra]
the day after tomorrow	**паслязаўтра** [paslʲaˈzawtra]
in the morning	**раніцай** [ranitsaj]
in the afternoon	**удзень** [uˈdzenʲ]
in the evening	**увечары** [uˈvetʃari]

aisle seat

window seat

How much?

Can I pay by credit card?

месца ля праходу
[mesʲtsa lʲa pra'hɔdu]

месца ля вакна
[mesʲtsa lʲa vak'na]

Колькі?
[kɔlʲki?]

Магу я заплаціць карткай?
[ma'hu ʲa zapla'tsitsʲ 'kartkaj?]

Bus

bus	**аўтобус** [aw'tɔbus]
intercity bus	**міжгародны аўтобус** [miʒɦa'rɔdnɨ aw'tɔbus]
bus stop	**аўтобусны прыпынак** [aw'tɔbusnɨ prɨ'pɨnak]
Where's the nearest bus stop?	**Дзе бліжэйшы аўтобусны прыпынак?** [dze bli'ʒɛjʃɨ aw'tɔbusnɨ prɨ'pɨnak?]
number (bus ~, etc.)	**нумар** [numar]
Which bus do I take to get to …?	**Які аўтобус ідзе да …?** [ʲaki aw'tɔbus i'dze da …?]
Does this bus go to …?	**Гэты аўтобус ідзе да …?** [ɦɛtɨ aw'tɔbus i'dze da …?]
How frequent are the buses?	**Як часта ходзяць аўтобусы?** [ʲak 'tʃasta 'hɔdzʲatsʲ aw'tɔbusɨ?]
every 15 minutes	**кожныя пятнаццаць хвілін** [kɔʒnʲʲa pʲat'natsatsʲ hvi'lin]
every half hour	**кожныя паўгадзіны** [kɔʒnʲʲa pawɦa'dzinɨ]
every hour	**кожную гадзіну** [kɔʒnuʉ ɦa'dzinu]
several times a day	**некалькі разоў на дзень** [nekalʲki ra'zɔw na dzenʲ]
… times a day	**… раз на дзень** [… raz na dzenʲ]
schedule	**расклад руху** [ras'klad 'ruhu]
Where can I see the schedule?	**Дзе можна паглядзець расклад руху?** [dze 'mɔʒna paɦlʲa'dzetsʲ ras'klad 'ruhu?]
When is the next bus?	**Калі будзе наступны аўтобус?** [ka'li 'budze nas'tupnɨ aw'tɔbus?]
When is the first bus?	**Калі адыходзіць першы аўтобус?** [ka'li adɨ'hɔdzitsʲ 'perʃɨ aw'tɔbus?]
When is the last bus?	**Калі адыходзіць апошні аўтобус?** [ka'li adɨ'hɔdzitsʲ a'pɔʃni aw'tɔbus?]

stop	**прыпынак** [pri'pinak]
next stop	**наступны прыпынак** [na'stupni pri'pinak]
last stop (terminus)	**канцавы прыпынак** [kantsa'vɨ pri'pinak]
Stop here, please.	**Спыніце тут, калі ласка.** [spi'nitse tut, ka'li 'laska.]
Excuse me, this is my stop.	**Дазвольце, гэта мой прыпынак.** [daz'volʲtse, 'ɦɛta mɔj pri'pinak.]

Train

train	цягнік [tsʲaĥ'nik]
suburban train	прыгарадны цягнік [priĥaradnɨ tsʲaĥ'nik]
long-distance train	цягнік дальняга следавання [tsʲaĥ'nik 'dalʲnʲaĥa 'sledavannʲa]
train station	вакзал [vak'zal]
Excuse me, where is the exit to the platform?	Прабачце, дзе выхад да цягнікоў? [pra'batʃtse, dze 'vɨhad da tsʲaĥni'kɔw?]
Does this train go to ...?	Гэты цягнік ідзе да ...? [ɦɛtɨ tsʲaĥ'nik i'dze da ...?]
next train	наступны цягнік [na'stupnɨ tsʲaĥ'nik]
When is the next train?	Калі будзе наступны цягнік? [kali 'budze na'stupnɨ tsʲaĥ'nik?]
Where can I see the schedule?	Дзе можна паглядзець расклад руху? [dze 'mɔʒna paĥlʲa'dzetsʲ ras'klad 'ruhu?]
From which platform?	Ад якой платформы? [at 'ʲakɔj plat'fɔrmɨ?]
When does the train arrive in ...?	Калі цягнік прыбудзе ў ...? [kali tsʲaĥ'nik pri'budze w ...?]
Please help me.	Дапамажыце мне, калі ласка. [dapama'ʒɨtse mne, ka'li 'laska.]
I'm looking for my seat.	Я шукаю сваё месца. [ʲa ʃu'kau svaʲo 'mesʲtsa.]
We're looking for our seats.	Мы шукаем нашыя месцы. [mɨ ʃu'kaem 'naʃʲʲa 'mesʲtsɨ.]
My seat is taken.	Маё месца занята. [maʲo 'mesʲtsa za'nʲata.]
Our seats are taken.	Нашыя месцы занятыя. [naʃʲʲa 'mesʲtsɨ za'nʲati.]
I'm sorry but this is my seat.	Прабачце, калі ласка, але гэта маё месца. [pra'batʃtse, ka'li 'laska, ale 'ɦɛta maʲo 'mesʲtsa.]

Is this seat taken? **Гэта месца свабодна?**
[ɦɛta 'mesʲtsa svaˈbɔdna?]

May I sit here? **Магу я тут сесці?**
[maˈɦu ʲa tut 'sesʲtsi?]

On the train. Dialogue (No ticket)

Ticket, please.
Ваш білет, калі ласка.
[vaʃ bi'let, ka'li 'laska.]

I don't have a ticket.
У мяне няма білета.
[u mʲa'ne nʲa'ma bi'leta.]

I lost my ticket.
Я згубіў /згубіла/ свой білет.
[ʲa zɦu'biw /zɦu'bila/ svɔj bi'let.]

I forgot my ticket at home.
Я забыўся /забылася/ білет дома.
[ʲa za'biwsʲa /za'bilasʲa/ bi'let 'dɔma.]

You can buy a ticket from me.
Вы можаце купіць білет у мяне.
[vɨ 'mɔʒatse ku'pitsʲ bi'let u mʲa'ne.]

You will also have to pay a fine.
Вам яшчэ давядзецца заплаціць штраф.
[vam ʲaɕɛ davʲa'dzɛtsa zapla'tsitsʲ 'ʃtraf.]

Okay.
Добра.
[dɔbra.]

Where are you going?
Куды вы едзеце?
[ku'dɨ vɨ 'edzetse?]

I'm going to …
Я еду да …
[ʲa 'edu da …]

How much? I don't understand.
Колькі? Я не разумею.
[kɔlʲki? ʲa ne razu'meʉ.]

Write it down, please.
Напішыце, калі ласка.
[napi'ʃɨtse, ka'li 'laska.]

Okay. Can I pay with a credit card?
Добра. Магу я заплаціць карткай?
[dɔbra. ma'ɦu ʲa zapla'tsitsʲ 'kartkaj?]

Yes, you can.
Так, можаце.
[tak, 'mɔʒatse.]

Here's your receipt.
Вось ваш квіток.
[vɔsʲ vaʃ kvi'tɔk.]

Sorry about the fine.
Спачуваю наконт штрафу.
[spatʃu'vaʉ na'kɔnt 'ʃtrafu.]

That's okay. It was my fault.
Гэта нічога. Гэта мая віна.
[ɦɛta ni'tʃɔɦa 'ɦɛta maʲa 'vina.]

Enjoy your trip.
Прыемнай вам паездкі!
[pri'emnaj vam pa'eztki.]

Taxi

taxi	**таксі** [tak'si]
taxi driver	**таксіст** [tak'sist]
to catch a taxi	**злавіць таксі** [zla'vitsʲ tak'si]
taxi stand	**стаянка таксі** [sta'ʲanka tak'si]
Where can I get a taxi?	**Дзе я магу ўзяць таксі?** [dze ʲa ma'ɦu wzʲatsʲ tak'si?]

to call a taxi	**выклікаць таксі** [viklikatsʲ tak'si]
I need a taxi.	**Мне патрэбна таксі.** [mne pa'trɛbna tak'si.]
Right now.	**Дакладна зараз.** [da'kladna 'zaraz.]
What is your address (location)?	**Ваш адрас?** [vaʃ 'adras?]
My address is ...	**Мой адрас ...** [mɔj 'adras ...]
Your destination?	**Куды вы паедзеце?** [ku'dɨ vɨ pa'edzetse?]

Excuse me, ...	**Прабачце, ...** [pra'batʃtse, ...]
Are you available?	**Вы свабодныя?** [vɨ sva'bɔdnɨʲa?]
How much is it to get to ...?	**Колькі каштуе даехаць да ...?** [kɔlʲki kaʃ'tue da'ehatsʲ da ...?]
Do you know where it is?	**Вы ведаеце, дзе гэта?** [vɨ 'vedaetse, dze 'ɦɛta?]

Airport, please.	**У аэрапорт, калі ласка.** [u aɛra'pɔrt, ka'li 'laska.]
Stop here, please.	**Спыніце тут, калі ласка.** [spɨ'nitse tut, ka'li 'laska.]
It's not here.	**Гэта ня тут.** [ɦɛta nʲa tut.]
This is the wrong address.	**Гэта няправільны адрас.** [ɦɛta nʲa'pravilʲnɨ 'adras.]
Turn left.	**Зараз налева.** [zaraz na'leva.]

Turn right. | **Зараз направа.**
[zaraz na'prava.]

How much do I owe you? | **Колькі я вам павінен /павінна/ заплаціць?**
[kɔlʲki ʲa vam pa'vinen /pa'vinna/ zapla'tsitsʲ?]

I'd like a receipt, please. | **Дайце мне квіток, калі ласка.**
[dajtse mne kvi'tɔk, ka'li 'laska.]

Keep the change. | **Рэшты ня трэба.**
[rɛʃtɨ nʲa 'trɛba.]

Would you please wait for me? | **Пачакайце мяне, калі ласка.**
[patʃa'kajtse mʲa'ne, ka'li 'laska.]

five minutes | **пяць хвілін**
[pʲatsʲ hvi'lin]

ten minutes | **дзесяць хвілін**
[dzesʲatsʲ hvi'lin]

fifteen minutes | **пятнаццаць хвілін**
[pʲat'natsatsʲ hvi'lin]

twenty minutes | **дваццаць хвілін**
[dvatsatsʲ hvi'lin]

half an hour | **паўгадзіны**
[pawɦa'dzinɨ]

Hotel

Hello.	**Прывітанне.** [privi'tanne.]
My name is ...	**Мяне завуць ...** [mʲaˈne zaˈvutsʲ ...]
I have a reservation.	**Я зарэзерваваў /зарэзервавала/ нумар.** [ʲa zarɛzervaˈvaw /zarɛzervaˈvala/ ˈnumar.]
I need ...	**Мне патрэбны ...** [mne paˈtrɛbnɨ ...]
a single room	**аднамесны нумар** [adnaˈmesnɨ ˈnumar]
a double room	**двухмесны нумар** [dvuhˈmesnɨ ˈnumar]
How much is that?	**Колькі ён каштуе?** [kɔlʲki ʲon kaʃˈtue?]
That's a bit expensive.	**Гэта крыху дорага.** [ɦɛta ˈkrɨhu ˈdoraɦa.]
Do you have anything else?	**У вас ёсць яшчэ што-небудзь?** [u vas ʲostsʲ ʲaˈɕɛ ʃtɔ ˈnebutsʲ?]
I'll take it.	**Я вазьму.** [ʲa vazʲˈmu.]
I'll pay in cash.	**Я заплачу наяўнымі.** [ʲa zaplaˈtʃu naˈʲawnɨmi.]
I've got a problem.	**У мяне ёсць праблема** [u mʲaˈne ʲostsʲ prabˈlema.]
My ... is out of order.	**У мяне не працуе ...** [u mʲaˈne ne praˈtsue ...]
TV	**тэлевізар** [teleˈvizar]
air conditioner	**кандыцыянер** [kandɨtsiʲaˈner]
tap	**кран** [kran]
shower	**душ** [duʃ]
sink	**ракавіна** [rakaˈvina]
safe	**сейф** [sejf]

door lock	**замок** [za'mɔk]
electrical outlet	**разетка** [ra'zetka]
hairdryer	**фен** [fen]

I don't have …	**У мяне няма …** [u mʲa'ne nʲa'ma …]
water	**вады** [va'dɨ]
light	**святла** [svʲat'la]
electricity	**электрычнасці** [ɛlekt'ritʃnasʲtsi]

Can you give me …?	**Можаце мне даць …?** [mɔʒatse mne datsʲ …?]
a towel	**рушнік** [ruʃʲnik]
a blanket	**коўдру** [kɔwdru]
slippers	**тапачкі** [tapatʃki]
a robe	**халат** [ha'lat]
shampoo	**шампунь** [ʃam'punʲ]
soap	**мыла** [mɨla]

I'd like to change rooms.	**Я б хацеў /хацела б/ памяняць нумар.** [ʲa b ha'tsew /ha'tsela/ pamʲa'nʲatsʲ 'numar.]
I can't find my key.	**Я не магу знайсці свой ключ.** [ʲa ne ma'ɦu znajsʲtsi svɔj klutʃ.]
Could you open my room, please?	**Адчыніце мой нумар, калі ласка.** [attʃɨ'nitse mɔj 'numar, ka'li 'laska.]

Who's there?	**Хто там?** [htɔ tam?]
Come in!	**Увайдзіце!** [uvaj'dzitse!]
Just a minute!	**Адну хвіліну!** [ad'nu hvi'linu!]

Not right now, please.	**Калі ласка, ня зараз.** [ka'li 'laska, nʲa 'zaraz.]
Come to my room, please.	**Зайдзіце да мяне, калі ласка.** [zaj'dzitse da mʲa'ne, ka'li 'laska.]

I'd like to order food service.

Я хачу замовіць ежу ў нумар.
[ˈa haˈtʃu zaˈmɔwitsʲ ˈeʒu w ˈnumar.]

My room number is …

Нумар майго пакоя …
[numar majˈɦɔ paˈkɔʲa …]

I'm leaving …

Я з'язджаю …
[ˈa zʲazˈdʒau …]

We're leaving …

Мы з'язджаем …
[mɨ zʲazˈdʒaem …]

right now

зараз
[zaraz]

this afternoon

сёння пасля абеду
[sʲonnʲa pasˈlʲa aˈbedu]

tonight

сёння ўвечары
[sʲonnʲa uˈwetʃarʲ]

tomorrow

заўтра
[zawtra]

tomorrow morning

заўтра ўранку
[zawtra uˈranku]

tomorrow evening

заўтра ўвечары
[zawtra uˈwetʃarʲ]

the day after tomorrow

паслязаўтра
[paslʲaˈzawtra]

I'd like to pay.

Я б хацеў /хацела б/ разлічыцца.
[ˈa b haˈtsew /haˈtsela/ razliˈtʃɨtsa.]

Everything was wonderful.

Усё было выдатна.
[wsʲo bɨˈlo vɨˈdatna.]

Where can I get a taxi?

Дзе я магу ўзяць таксі?
[dze ʲa maˈɦu wzʲatsʲ takˈsi?]

Would you call a taxi for me, please?

Выклікайце мне таксі, калі ласка.
[vɨklikajtse mne taksi, kaˈli ˈlaska.]

Restaurant

Can I look at the menu, please?	**Магу я паглядзець ваша меню?** [ma'hu ɪa pahlɪa'dzetsɪ 'vaʃa me'nʉ?]
Table for one.	**Столік для аднаго.** [stolik dlɪa adna'ɦɔ.]
There are two (three, four) of us.	**Нас два (тры, чатыры) чалавекі.** [nas dva (trɪ, tʃa'tɪrɪ) tʃala'veki.]

Smoking	**Для тых, хто паліць.** [dlɪa tiɦ, htɔ 'palitsɪ]
No smoking	**Для тых, хто ня паліць.** [dlɪa tiɦ, htɔ nɪa 'palitsɪ]
Excuse me! (addressing a waiter)	**Будзьце ласкавы!** [butɪtse las'kaviɪ]
menu	**меню** [me'nʉ]
wine list	**карта він** [karta vin]
The menu, please.	**Меню, калі ласка.** [me'nʉ, ka'li 'laska.]

Are you ready to order?	**Вы гатовы зрабіць замову?** [vɪ ɦa'tɔvɪ zra'bitsɪ za'mɔvu?]
What will you have?	**Што вы будзеце замаўляць?** [ʃtɔ vɪ 'budzetse zamaw'lɪatsɪ?]
I'll have …	**Я буду …** [ɪa 'budu …]

I'm a vegetarian.	**Я вегетарыянец /вегетарыянка/.** [ɪa veɦetari'ɪanets /veɦetari'ɪanka/.]
meat	**мяса** [mɪasa]
fish	**рыба** [riba]
vegetables	**гародніна** [ɦa'rɔdnina]
Do you have vegetarian dishes?	**У вас ёсць вегетарыянскія стравы?** [u vas ɪɔstsɪ veɦetari'ɪanskiɪa 'stravɪ?]
I don't eat pork.	**Я ня ем свініну.** [ɪa nɪa em svi'ninu.]
He /she/ doesn't eat meat.	**Ён /яна/ не есць мяса.** [ɪɔn /ɪa'na/ ne estsɪ 'mɪasa.]
I am allergic to …	**У мяне алергія на …** [u mɪa'ne aler'ɦiɪa na …]

Would you please bring me ...
Прынясіце мне, калі ласка ...
[prinʲa'siʦe mne, ka'li 'laska ...]

salt | pepper | sugar
соль | перац | цукар
[sɔlʲ | 'peraʦ | 'ʦukar]

coffee | tea | dessert
каву | гарбату | дэсерт
[kavu | ɦar'batu | dɛ'sert]

water | sparkling | plain
вада | з газам | бяз газу
[va'da | z 'ɦazam | bʲaz 'ɦazu]

a spoon | fork | knife
лыжка | відэлец | нож
[liʒka | vi'dɛleʦ | nɔʒ]

a plate | napkin
талерка | сурвэтка
[ta'lerka | sur'vɛtka]

Enjoy your meal!
Прыемнага апетыту!
[pri'emnaɦa ape'titu!]

One more, please.
Прынясіце яшчэ, калі ласка.
[prinʲa'siʦe ʲa'ɕɛ, ka'li 'laska.]

It was very delicious.
Было вельмі смачна.
[bi'lɔ 'velʲmi 'smaʧna.]

check | change | tip
рахунак | рэшта | на гарбату
[ra'ɦunak | 'rɛʃta | na ɦar'batu]

Check, please.
(Could I have the check, please?)
Рахунак, калі ласка.
[ra'ɦunak, ka'li 'laska.]

Can I pay by credit card?
Магу я заплаціць карткай?
[ma'ɦu ʲa zapla'ʦiʦʲ 'kartkaj?]

I'm sorry, there's a mistake here.
Прабачце, тут памылка.
[pra'baʧʦe, tut pa'milka.]

Shopping

Can I help you?	**Магу я вам дапамагчы?** [ma'ɦu ʲa vam dapamaɦ'tʃɨ?]
Do you have …?	**У вас ёсць …?** [u vas ʲosʲtsʲ …?]
I'm looking for …	**Я шукаю …** [ʲa ʃu'kaʉ …]
I need …	**Мне патрэбны …** [mne pa'trɛbnɨ …]
I'm just looking.	**Я проста гляджу.** [ʲa 'prɔsta ɦlʲa'dʒu.]
We're just looking.	**Мы проста глядзім.** [mɨ 'prɔsta ɦlʲa'dzim.]
I'll come back later.	**Я зайду пазней.** [ʲa zaj'du paz'nej.]
We'll come back later.	**Мы зойдзем пазней.** [mɨ 'zɔjdzem paz'nej.]
discounts	sale	**зніжкі	распродаж** [zniʒki	ras'prɔdaʒ]
Would you please show me …	**Пакажыце мне, калі ласка …** [paka'ʒɨtse mne, ka'li 'laska …]
Would you please give me …	**Дайце мне, калі ласка …** [dajtse mne, ka'li 'laska …]
Can I try it on?	**Магу я гэта прымерыць?** [ma'ɦu ʲa 'ɦɛta prɨ'merɨtsʲ?]
Excuse me, where's the fitting room?	**Прабачце, дзе прымерачная кабіна?** [pra'batʃtse, dze prɨ'meratʃnaʲa ka'bina?]
Which color would you like?	**Які колер вы жадаеце?** [ʲaki 'kɔler vɨ ʒa'daetse?]
size	length	**памер	рост** [pa'mer	rɔst]
How does it fit?	**Падыйшло?** [padɨj'ʃlɔ?]
How much is it?	**Колькі гэта каштуе?** [kɔlʲki 'ɦɛta kaʃ'tue?]
That's too expensive.	**Гэта занадта дорага.** [ɦɛta za'natta 'dɔraɦa.]
I'll take it.	**Я вазьму гэта.** [ʲa vazʲ'mu 'ɦɛta.]
Excuse me, where do I pay?	**Прабачце, дзе каса?** [pra'batʃtse, dze 'kasa?]

Will you pay in cash or credit card?

Як вы будзеце разлічвацца? Наяўнымі ці крэдытнай карткай?
['ak vɨ 'budʑetse raz'litʃvatsa naᶥawnɨmi tsi krɛ'dɨtnaj 'kartkaj?]

In cash | with credit card

наяўнымі | карткай
[naᶥawnɨmi | 'kartkaj]

Do you want the receipt?

Вам патрэбен квіток?
[vam pa'trɛben kvi'tɔk?]

Yes, please.

Так, будзьце ласкавы.
[tak, 'butᶥtse las'kavɨ.]

No, it's OK.

Не. Не патрэбен. Дзякуй.
[ne, ne pa'trɛben. 'dʑakuj.]

Thank you. Have a nice day!

Дзякуй. Усяго добрага!
[dʑᶥakuj. usᶥa'hɔ 'dɔbraɦa!]

In town

Excuse me, please.	**Прабачце, калі ласка …** [pra'batʃtse, ka'li 'laska …]
I'm looking for …	**Я шукаю …** [ʲa ʃu'kau̯ …]

the subway	**метро** [me'trɔ]
my hotel	**сваю гасцініцу** [sva'u̯ ɦas'tsinitsu]
the movie theater	**кінатэатр** [kinatɛ'atr]
a taxi stand	**стаянку таксі** [sta'ʲanku tak'si]

an ATM	**банкамат** [banka'mat]
a foreign exchange office	**пункт абмену валют** [punkt ab'menu va'lu̯t]
an internet café	**інтэрнэт-кафэ** [intɛr'nɛt ka'fɛ]
… street	**вуліцу …** [vulitsu …]
this place	**вось гэтае месца** [vɔsʲ 'ɦɛtae 'mesʲtsa]

Do you know where … is?	**Вы ня ведаеце, дзе знаходзіцца …?** [vɨ nʲa 'vedaetse, dze zna'ɦɔdzitsa …?]
Which street is this?	**Як называецца гэтая вуліца?** [ʲak nazɨ'vaetsa 'ɦɛtaʲa 'vulitsa?]
Show me where we are right now.	**Пакажыце, дзе мы зараз.** [paka'ʒɨtse, dze mɨ 'zaraz.]

Can I get there on foot?	**Я дайду туды пешшу?** [ʲa daj'du tu'dɨ 'peʃu?]
Do you have a map of the city?	**У вас ёсць карта горада?** [u vas ʲosʲtsʲ 'karta 'ɦɔrada?]

How much is a ticket to get in?	**Колькі каштуе ўваходны білет?** [kɔlʲki kaʃ'tue wva'ɦɔdnɨ bi'let?]
Can I take pictures here?	**Тут дазволена фатаграфаваць?** [tut daz'vɔlena fataɦrafa'vatsʲ?]
Are you open?	**Вы адчынены?** [vɨ at'ʧɨnenɨ?]

When do you open?

А якой гадзіне вы адчыняецеся?
[a ˈjakɔj ɦaˈdzine vɨ atʧɨˈnʲaetsesʲa?]

When do you close?

Да якой гадзіны вы працуеце?
[da ʲaˈkɔj ɦaˈdzinɨ vɨ praˈtsuetse?]

Money

money	**грошы** [ɦrɔʃi]
cash	**наяўныя грошы** [naˈʲawnʲʲa ˈɦrɔʃi]
paper money	**папяровыя грошы** [papʲaˈrovʲʲa ˈɦrɔʃi]
loose change	**дробязь** [drɔbʲazʲ]
check | change | tip	**рахунак | рэшта | на гарбату** [raˈhunak | ˈrɛʃta | na ɦarˈbatu]

credit card	**крэдытная картка** [krɛˈdʲtnaʲa ˈkartka]
wallet	**кашалёк** [kaʃaˈlʲok]
to buy	**купляць** [kupˈlʲatsʲ]
to pay	**плаціць** [plaˈtsʲitsʲ]
fine	**штраф** [ʃtraf]
free	**бясплатна** [bʲasˈplatna]

Where can I buy ...?	**Дзе я магу купіць ...?** [dze ʲa maˈɦu kuˈpʲitsʲ ...?]
Is the bank open now?	**Банк зараз адчынены?** [bank ˈzaraz atˈʧineni?]
When does it open?	**А якой гадзіне ён адчыняецца?** [a ˈʲakɔj ɦaˈdzine ʲon atʧʲiˈnʲaeʦa?]
When does it close?	**Да якой гадзіны ён працуе?** [da ʲaˈkɔj ɦaˈdzini ʲon praˈtsue?]

How much?	**Колькі?** [kɔlʲki?]
How much is this?	**Колькі гэта каштуе?** [kɔlʲki ˈɦɛta kaʃˈtue?]
That's too expensive.	**Гэта занадта дорага.** [ˈɦɛta zaˈnatta ˈdɔraɦa.]

| Excuse me, where do I pay? | **Прабачце, дзе каса?**
[praˈbaʧtse, dze ˈkasa?] |
| Check, please. | **Рахунак, калі ласка.**
[raˈhunak, kaˈli ˈlaska.] |

Can I pay by credit card?

Магу я заплаціць карткай?
[ma'ɦu ʲa zapla'tsitsʲ 'kartkaj?]

Is there an ATM here?

Тут ёсць банкамат?
[tut ʲostsʲ banka'mat?]

I'm looking for an ATM.

Мне патрэбен банкамат.
[mne pa'trɛben banka'mat.]

I'm looking for a foreign exchange office.

Я шукаю пункт абмену валют.
[ʲa ʃu'kaju punkt ab'menu va'lʉt.]

I'd like to change ...

Я б хацеў /хацела/ памяняць ...
[ʲa b ha'tsew /ha'tsela/ pamʲa'nʲatsʲ ...]

What is the exchange rate?

Які курс абмену?
[ʲaki kurs ab'menu?]

Do you need my passport?

Вам патрэбен мой пашпарт?
[vam pa'trɛben mɔj 'paʃpart?]

Time

What time is it?	**Колькі часу?** [kolʲki 'tʃasu?]
When?	**Калі?** [ka'li?]
At what time?	**У колькі?** [u 'kolʲki?]
now | later | after …	**зараз | пазней | пасля …** [zaraz | paz'nej | pas'lʲa …]
one o'clock	**гадзіна папоўдні** [ɦa'dzina pa'powdni]
one fifteen	**гадзіна пятнаццаць** [ɦa'dzina pʲat'natsatsʲ]
one thirty	**гадзіна трыццаць** [ɦa'dzina 'tritsatsʲ]
one forty-five	**без пятнаццаці два** [bez pʲat'natsatsi dva]
one | two | three	**адзін | два | тры** [a'dzin | dva | trɨ]
four | five | six	**чатыры | пяць | шэсць** [tʃa'tirɨ | pʲatsʲ | ʃɛstsʲ]
seven | eight | nine	**сем | восем | дзевяць** [sem | 'vosem | 'dzevʲatsʲ]
ten | eleven | twelve	**дзесяць | адзінаццаць | дванаццаць** [dzesʲatsʲ | a'dzinatsatsʲ | dva'natsatsʲ]
in …	**праз …** [praz …]
five minutes	**пяць хвілін** [pʲatsʲ hvi'lin]
ten minutes	**дзесяць хвілін** [dzesʲatsʲ hvi'lin]
fifteen minutes	**пятнаццаць хвілін** [pʲat'natsatsʲ hvi'lin]
twenty minutes	**дваццаць хвілін** [dvatsatsʲ hvi'lin]
half an hour	**паўгадзіны** [pawɦa'dzinɨ]
an hour	**адну гадзіну** [ad'nu ɦa'dzinu]
in the morning	**раніцай, уранні** [ranitsaj, u'ranni]
early in the morning	**рана ўранні** [rana u'ranni]

this morning	сёння ўдзень [sʲonnʲa u'dzenʲ]
tomorrow morning	заўтра раніцай [zawtra 'ranitsaj]

in the middle of the day	у абед [u a'bet]
in the afternoon	пасля абеду [pasʲlʲa a'bedu]
in the evening	увечары [u'vetʃarɨ]
tonight	сёння увечары [sʲonnʲa u'vetʃarɨ]

at night	ноччу [notʃu]
yesterday	учора [u'tʃora]
today	сёння [sʲonnʲa]
tomorrow	заўтра [zawtra]
the day after tomorrow	паслязаўтра [pasʲlʲa'zawtra]

What day is it today?	Які сёння дзень? [ʲaki 'sʲonnʲa dzenʲ?]
It's …	Сёння … [sʲonnʲa …]
Monday	панядзелак [panʲa'dzelak]
Tuesday	аўторак [aw'torak]
Wednesday	серада [sera'da]

Thursday	чацвер [tʃats'ver]
Friday	пятніца [pʲatnitsa]
Saturday	субота [su'bota]
Sunday	нядзеля [nʲa'dzelʲa]

Greetings. Introductions

Hello.	**Прывітанне.** [privi'tanne.]
Pleased to meet you.	**Рады /рада/ з вамі пазнаёміцца.** [radɨ /'rada/ z 'vami paznaⁱomitsa.]
Me too.	**Я таксама.** [ⁱa tak'sama.]
I'd like you to meet ...	**Знаёмцеся. Гэта ...** [znaⁱomtsesⁱa. 'ɦɛta ...]
Nice to meet you.	**Вельмі прыемна.** [velⁱmi pri'emna.]

How are you?	**Як вашы справы?** [ⁱak 'vaʃɨ 'spravɨ?]
My name is ...	**Мяне завуць ...** [mⁱa'ne za'vutsⁱ ...]
His name is ...	**Яго завуць ...** [ⁱaɦɔ za'vutsⁱ ...]
Her name is ...	**Яе завуць ...** [ⁱae za'vutsⁱ ...]

What's your name?	**Як вас завуць?** [ⁱak vas za'vutsⁱ?]
What's his name?	**Як яго завуць?** [ⁱak ⁱa'ɦɔ za'vutsⁱ?]
What's her name?	**Як яе завуць?** [ⁱak ⁱae za'vutsⁱ?]

What's your last name?	**Як ваша прозвішча?** [ⁱak 'vaʃa 'prɔzviʧa?]
You can call me ...	**Завіце мяне ...** [za'vitse mⁱa'ne ...]
Where are you from?	**Адкуль вы?** [at'kulⁱ vɨ]
I'm from ...	**Я з ...** [ⁱa z ...]
What do you do for a living?	**Кім вы працуеце?** [kim vɨ pra'tsuetse?]

Who is this?	**Хто гэта?** [htɔ 'ɦɛta?]
Who is he?	**Хто ён?** [htɔ ⁱon?]
Who is she?	**Хто яна?** [htɔ ⁱa'na?]

Who are they?	**Хто яны?** [htɔ ʲaˈnʲi?]
This is ...	**Гэта ...** [hɛta ...]
my friend (masc.)	**мой сябар** [mɔj ˈsʲabar]
my friend (fem.)	**мая сяброўка** [maˈʲa sʲabˈrɔwka]
my husband	**мой муж** [mɔj muʒ]
my wife	**мая жонка** [maˈʲa ˈʒɔnka]

my father	**мой бацька** [mɔj ˈbatsʲka]
my mother	**мая маці** [maˈʲa ˈmatsi]
my brother	**мой брат** [mɔj brat]
my sister	**мая сястра** [maˈʲa sʲasˈtra]
my son	**мой сын** [mɔj sʲin]
my daughter	**мая дачка** [maˈʲa datʃˈka]

This is our son.	**Гэта наш сын.** [hɛta naʃ sʲin.]
This is our daughter.	**Гэта наша дачка.** [hɛta ˈnaʃa datʃˈka.]
These are my children.	**Гэта мае дзеці.** [hɛta mae ˈdzetsi.]
These are our children.	**Гэта нашы дзеці.** [hɛta naʃɨ ˈdzetsi.]

Farewells

Good bye!	**Да пабачэння!** [da paba'ʧɛnnʲa!]
Bye! (inform.)	**Бывай!** [bi'vaj!]
See you tomorrow.	**Да заўтра.** [da 'zawtra.]
See you soon.	**Да сустрэчы.** [da sus'trɛʧi.]
See you at seven.	**Сустрэнемся ў сем.** [sus'trɛnemsʲa w sem.]

Have fun!	**Баўцеся!** [bawʦesʲa!]
Talk to you later.	**Пагаворым пазней.** [paɦa'vɔrim paz'nej.]
Have a nice weekend.	**Удалых выхадных.** [u'dalih vihad'nih.]
Good night.	**Дабранач.** [da'branaʧ.]

It's time for me to go.	**Мне трэба ісці.** [mne 'trɛba is'ʦi.]
I have to go.	**Мне трэба ісці.** [mne 'trɛba is'ʦi.]
I will be right back.	**Я зараз вярнуся.** [ʲa 'zaraz vʲar'nusʲa.]

It's late.	**Ужо позна.** [uʒɔ 'pɔzna.]
I have to get up early.	**Мне рана ўставаць.** [mne 'rana wsta'vaʦʲ.]
I'm leaving tomorrow.	**Я заўтра з'язджаю.** [ʲa 'zawtra zʲaz'ʤau.]
We're leaving tomorrow.	**Мы заўтра з'язджаем.** [mi 'zawtra zʲaz'ʤaem.]

Have a nice trip!	**Шчаслівай паездкі!** [ɕas'livaj pa'eztki!]
It was nice meeting you.	**Было прыемна з вамі пазнаёміцца.** [bi'lɔ pri'emna z 'vami pazna'ʲomiʦa.]
It was nice talking to you.	**Было прыемна з вамі пагутарыць.** [bi'lɔ pri'emna z 'vami pa'ɦutariʦʲ.]
Thanks for everything.	**Дзякуй за ўсё.** [dzʲakuj za 'wsʲo.]

I had a very good time.	**Я цудоўна збавіў /збавіла/ час!** ['a ʦu'dɔwna 'zbawiw /'zbawila/ ʧas.]
We had a very good time.	**Мы цудоўна збавілі час!** [mɨ ʦu'dɔwna 'zbawili ʧas.]
It was really great.	**Усё было выдатна.** [wsʲo bɨ'lɔ vɨ'datna.]
I'm going to miss you.	**Я буду сумаваць.** ['a 'budu suma'vatsʲ.]
We're going to miss you.	**Мы будзем сумаваць.** [mɨ 'budzem suma'vatsʲ.]
Good luck!	**Удачы! Шчасліва!** [u'datʃɨ! ɕas'liva!]
Say hi to …	**Перадавайце прывітанне ...** [perada'vajʦe privi'tanne …]

Foreign language

I don't understand.	**Я не разумею.**
	[ˈʲa ne razuˈmeʉ.]
Write it down, please.	**Напішыце гэта, калі ласка.**
	[napiˈʂɨtse ˈɦɛta, kaˈli ˈlaska.]
Do you speak …?	**Вы валодаеце …?**
	[vɨ vaˈlɔdaetse …?]

I speak a little bit of …	**Я крыху валодаю … мовай**
	[ˈʲa ˈkrɨhu vaˈlɔdaʉ … ˈmɔvaj]
English	**англійскай**
	[anɦˈlijskaj]
Turkish	**турэцкай**
	[tuˈrɛtskaj]
Arabic	**арабскай**
	[aˈrabskaj]
French	**французкай**
	[franˈtsuskaj]

German	**нямецкай**
	[nʲaˈmetskaj]
Italian	**італьянскай**
	[itaˈlʲanskaj]
Spanish	**іспанскай**
	[isˈpanskaj]
Portuguese	**партугальскай**
	[partuˈɦalʲskaj]
Chinese	**кітайскай**
	[kiˈtajskaj]
Japanese	**японскай**
	[ˈʲaˈpɔnskaj]

Can you repeat that, please.	**Паўтарыце, калі ласка.**
	[pawtaˈritse, kaˈli ˈlaska.]
I understand.	**Я разумею.**
	[ˈʲa razuˈmeʉ.]
I don't understand.	**Я не разумею.**
	[ˈʲa ne razuˈmeʉ.]
Please speak more slowly.	**Гаварыце павольней, калі ласка.**
	[ɦavaˈritse paˈvɔlʲnej, kaˈli ˈlaska.]

Is that correct? (Am I saying it right?)	**Гэта правільна?**
	[ɦɛta ˈpravilʲna?]
What is this? (What does this mean?)	**Что гэта?**
	[tʃto ˈɦɛta?]

Apologies

Excuse me, please.	**Выбачайце, калі ласка.** [vɨbaˈtʃajtse, kaˈli ˈlaska.]
I'm sorry.	**Мне шкада.** [mne ˈʃkada.]
I'm really sorry.	**Мне вельмі шкада.** [mne ˈvelʲmi ˈʃkada.]
Sorry, it's my fault.	**Я вінаваты /вінавата/, гэта мая віна.** [ʲa vinaˈvatɨ /vinaˈvata/, ˈɦɛta maʲa ˈvina.]
My mistake.	**Мая памылка.** [maˈʲa paˈmɨɫka.]

May I ...?	**Магу я...?** [maˈɦu ʲa ...?]
Do you mind if I ...?	**Вы не будзеце пярэчыць, калі я ...?** [vɨ ne ˈbudzetse pʲaˈrɛtʃɨtsʲ, kaˈli ʲa ...?]
It's OK.	**Нічога страшнага.** [niˈtʃoɦa ˈstraʃnaɦa.]
It's all right.	**Усё ў парадку.** [wsʲo w paˈratku.]
Don't worry about it.	**Не хвалюйцеся.** [ne hvaˈlʲujtsesʲa.]

Agreement

Yes.	**Так.** [tak.]
Yes, sure.	**Так, канечне.** [tak, ka'netʃne.]
OK (Good!)	**Добра!** [dɔbra!]
Very well.	**Вельмі добра.** [velʲmi 'dɔbra.]
Certainly!	**Канечне!** [ka'netʃne!]
I agree.	**Я згодны /згодна/.** [ʲa 'zɦɔdni /'zɦɔdna/.]
That's correct.	**Дакладна.** [da'kladna.]
That's right.	**Правільна.** [pravilʲna.]
You're right.	**Вы маеце рацыю.** [vɨ 'maetse 'ratsɨʉ.]
I don't mind.	**Я ня супраць.** [ʲa nʲa 'supratsʲ.]
Absolutely right.	**Зусім дакладна.** [zu'sim da'kladna.]
It's possible.	**Гэта магчыма.** [ɦɛta maɦ'tʃima.]
That's a good idea.	**Гэта добрая думка.** [ɦɛta 'dɔbraʲa 'dumka.]
I can't say no.	**Не магу адмовіць.** [ne ma'ɦu ad'mɔvitsʲ.]
I'd be happy to.	**Буду рады /рада/.** [budu 'radɨ /'rada/.]
With pleasure.	**З задавальненнем.** [z zadavalʲ'nennem.]

Refusal. Expressing doubt

No.
Не.
[ne.]

Certainly not.
Канечне не.
[ka'netʃne ne.]

I don't agree.
Я не згодны /згодна/.
[ʲa ne 'zɦodnɨ /'zɦodna/.]

I don't think so.
Я так не лічу.
[ʲa tak ne li'tʃu.]

It's not true.
Гэта няпраўда.
[ɦɛta nʲa'prawda.]

You are wrong.
Вы памыляецеся.
[vɨ pamɨ'lʲaetsesʲa.]

I think you are wrong.
Я думаю, што вы памыляецеся.
[ʲa 'dumaʉ, ʃto vɨ pamɨ'lʲaetsesʲa.]

I'm not sure.
Не ўпэўнены /ўпэўнена/.
[ne u'pɛwnenɨ /u'pɛwnena/.]

It's impossible.
Гэта немагчыма.
[ɦɛta nemaɦ'tʃɨma.]

Nothing of the kind (sort)!
Нічога падобнага!
[ni'tʃoɦa pa'dobnaɦa!]

The exact opposite.
Наадварот!
[naadva'rɔt!]

I'm against it.
Я супраць.
[ʲa 'supratsʲ.]

I don't care.
Мне ўсё роўна.
[mne wsʲo 'rɔwna.]

I have no idea.
Паняцця ня маю.
[pa'nʲatsʲa nʲa 'maʉ.]

I doubt it.
Сумняваюся, что гэта так.
[sumnʲa'vaʉsʲa, tʃto 'ɦɛta tak.]

Sorry, I can't.
Прабачце, я не магу.
[pra'batʃtse, ʲa ne ma'ɦu.]

Sorry, I don't want to.
Прабачце, я не хачу.
[pra'batʃtse, ʲa ne ha'tʃu.]

Thank you, but I don't need this.
Дзякуй, мне гэта ня трэба.
[dzʲakuj, mne 'ɦɛta nʲa 'trɛba.]

It's getting late.
Ужо позна.
[uʒo 'pozna.]

I have to get up early.

Мне рана ўставаць.
[mne 'rana wsta'vatsʲ.]

I don't feel well.

Я дрэнна сябе адчуваю.
[ʲa 'drɛnna sʲa'be attʃu'vaʉ.]

Expressing gratitude

Thank you. — **Дзякуй.**
[dzʲakuj.]

Thank you very much. — **Дзякуй вялікі!**
[dzʲakuj vʲaˈliki.]

I really appreciate it. — **Вельмі ўдзячны /удзячна/.**
[welʲmi uˈdzʲatʃnʲi /uˈdzʲatʃna/.]

I'm really grateful to you. — **Я вам удзячны /удзячна/.**
[ˈja vam uˈdzʲatʃnʲi /uˈdzʲatʃna/.]

We are really grateful to you. — **Мы вам удзячны.**
[mɨ vam uˈdzʲatʃnʲi.]

Thank you for your time. — **Дзякуй, что выдаткавалі час.**
[dzʲakuj, tʃtɔ ˈvidatkavali tʃas.]

Thanks for everything. — **Дзякуй за ўсё.**
[dzʲakuj za ˈwsʲo.]

Thank you for ... — **Дзякуй за ...**
[dzʲakuj za ...]

your help — **вашу дапамогу**
[vaʃu dapaˈmɔɦu]

a nice time — **прыемныя часіны**
[priˈemnʲʲa tʃaˈsini]

a wonderful meal — **выдатную ежу**
[vʲiˈdatnuʉ ˈeʒu]

a pleasant evening — **прыемны вечар**
[priˈemnʲi ˈvetʃar]

a wonderful day — **цудоўны дзень**
[tsuˈdɔwnʲi dzenʲ]

an amazing journey — **цікавую экскурсію**
[tsiˈkavuʉ ɛksˈkursiʉ]

Don't mention it. — **Няма за што.**
[nʲaˈma za ˈʃtɔ.]

You are welcome. — **Ня варта падзякі.**
[nʲa ˈvarta paˈdzʲaki.]

Any time. — **Заўсёды калі ласка.**
[zawˈsʲodi kaˈli ˈlaska.]

My pleasure. — **Быў рады /Была рада/ дапамагчы.**
[bɨw ˈradi /bɨla ˈrada/ dapamaɦˈtʃi.]

Forget it. — **Забудзьце. Усё добра.**
[zaˈbutʲtse. wsʲo ˈdɔbra.]

Don't worry about it. — **Не турбуйцеся.**
[ne turˈbujtsesʲa.]

Congratulations. Best wishes

Congratulations!	Віншую! [vin'ʃuɥ!]
Happy birthday!	З днём нараджэння! [z 'dnʲom nara'dʒɛnnʲa!]
Merry Christmas!	Вясёлых Калядаў! [vʲa'sʲolɨh ka'lʲadaw!]
Happy New Year!	С Новым годам! [s 'nɔvɨm 'ɦɔdam!]

Happy Easter!	Са Светлым Вялікаднем! [sa 'svetlɨm vʲa'likadnem!]
Happy Hanukkah!	Счаслівай Хануці! [stʃas'livaj 'hanuki!]

I'd like to propose a toast.	У мяне ёсць тост. [u mʲa'ne ʲostsʲ tɔst.]
Cheers!	За ваша здароўе! [za 'vaʃa zda'rɔwe!]
Let's drink to …!	Вып'ем за …! [vʲp'em za …!]
To our success!	За нашыя поспехі! [za 'naʃʲa 'pɔspehi!]
To your success!	За вашыя поспехі! [za 'vaʃʲa 'pɔspehi!]

Good luck!	Удачы! [u'datʃɨ!]
Have a nice day!	Прыемнага вам дня! [prɨ'emnaɦa vam dnʲa!]
Have a good holiday!	Добрага вам адпачынку! [dɔbraɦa vam adpa'tʃinku!]
Have a safe journey!	Удалай паездкі! [u'dalaj pa'eztki!]
I hope you get better soon!	Жадаю вам хуткай папраўкі! [ʒa'daɥ vam 'hutkaj pa'prawki!]

Socializing

Why are you sad?	**Чаму вы засмучаны?** [tʃa'mu vɨ zas'mutʃanɨ?]
Smile! Cheer up!	**Усміхніцеся!** [usmih'nitʲsesʲa!]
Are you free tonight?	**Вы не занятыя сёння ўвечары?** [vɨ ne za'nʲatʲija 'sʲonnʲa u'wetʃarɨ?]
May I offer you a drink?	**Магу я прапанаваць вам выпіць?** [ma'ɦu ʲa prapana'vatsʲ vam 'vɨpitsʲ?]
Would you like to dance?	**Ня хочаце патанцаваць?** [nʲa 'ɦotʃatse patantsa'vatsʲ?]
Let's go to the movies.	**Можа сходзім у кіно?** [moʒa 'sɦodzim u ki'no?]
May I invite you to ...?	**Магу я запрасіць вас у ...?** [ma'ɦu ʲa zapra'sitsʲ vas u ...?]
a restaurant	**рэстаран** [rɛsta'ran]
the movies	**кіно** [ki'no]
the theater	**тэатр** [tɛ'atr]
go for a walk	**на прагулку** [na pra'ɦulku]
At what time?	**У колькі?** [u 'kolʲki?]
tonight	**сёння увечары** [sʲonnʲa u'vetʃarɨ]
at six	**у шэсць гадзін** [u ʃɛstsʲ ɦa'dzin]
at seven	**у сем гадзін** [u sem ɦa'dzin]
at eight	**у восем гадзін** [u 'vosem ɦa'dzin]
at nine	**у дзевяць гадзін** [u 'dzevʲatsʲ ɦa'dzin]
Do you like it here?	**Вам тут падабаецца?** [vam tut pada'baetsa?]
Are you here with someone?	**Вы тут з кімсьці?** [vɨ tut z 'kimsʲtsi?]
I'm with my friend.	**Я з сябрам /сяброўкай/.** [ʲa z 'sʲabram /sʲab'rowkaj/.]

I'm with my friends.

Я з сябрамі.
['a z s'ab'rami.]

No, I'm alone.

Я адзін /адна/.
['a a'dzin /ad'na/.]

Do you have a boyfriend?

У цябе ёсць прыяцель?
[u ts'a'be 'osts' pri'¹atsel'?]

I have a boyfriend.

У мяне ёсць сябар.
[u m'a'ne 'osts' 's'abar.]

Do you have a girlfriend?

У цябе ёсць сяброўка?
[u ts'a'be 'osts' s'ab'rowka?]

I have a girlfriend.

У мяне ёсць дзяўчына.
[u m'a'ne 'osts' dz'aw'tʃina.]

Can I see you again?

Мы яшчэ сустрэнемся?
[mi 'a'cɛ sus'trɛnems'a?]

Can I call you?

Можна я табе пазваню?
[moʒna 'a ta'be pazva'nu?]

Call me. (Give me a call.)

Пазвані мне.
[pazva'ni mne.]

What's your number?

Які ў цябе нумар?
['aki u ts'a'be 'numar?]

I miss you.

Я сумую па табе.
['a su'muʉ pa ta'be.]

You have a beautiful name.

У вас вельмі прыгожае імя.
[u vas 'vel'mi pri'hoʒae i'm'a.]

I love you.

Я цябе кахаю.
['a ts'a'be ka'haʉ.]

Will you marry me?

Выходзь за мяне замуж.
[vi'hots' za m'a'ne 'zamuʒ.]

You're kidding!

Вы жартуеце!
[vi ʒar'tuetse!]

I'm just kidding.

Я проста жартую.
['a 'prɔsta ʒar'tuʉ.]

Are you serious?

Вы сур'ёзна?
[vi su'r'ʲozna?]

I'm serious.

Я сур'ёзна.
['a su'r'ʲozna.]

Really?!

Сапраўды?!
[sapraw'di?!]

It's unbelievable!

Гэта неверагодна!
[ɦɛta nevera'ɦodna]

I don't believe you.

Я вам ня веру.
['a vam n'a 'veru.]

I can't.

Я не магу.
['a ne ma'ɦu.]

I don't know.

Я ня ведаю.
['a n'a 'vedaʉ.]

I don't understand you.	**Я вас не разумею.** ['a vas ne razu'meʉ.]
Please go away.	**Сыдзіце, калі ласка.** [sɨ'dzitse, ka'li 'laska.]
Leave me alone!	**Пакіньце мяне у спакоі!** [pa'kinʲtse mʲa'ne u spa'kɔi!]

I can't stand him.	**Я яго не выношу!** ['a ʲa'hɔ ne vɨ'nɔʃu.]
You are disgusting!	**Вы агідныя!** [vɨ a'hidnʲa!]
I'll call the police!	**Я выклікаю міліцыю!** ['a 'vɨklikaʉ mi'litsʉ!]

Sharing impressions. Emotions

I like it.	**Мне гэта падабаецца.** [mne 'ɦɛta pada'baetsa.]
Very nice.	**Вельмі міла.** [velʲmi 'mila.]
That's great!	**Гэта выдатна!** [ɦɛta viˈdatna!]
It's not bad.	**Гэта някепска.** [ɦɛta nʲaˈkepska.]
I don't like it.	**Гэта мне не падабаецца** [ɦɛta mne ne padaˈbaetsa.]
It's not good.	**Гэта нядобра.** [ɦɛta nʲaˈdobra.]
It's bad.	**Гэта дрэнна.** [ɦɛta ˈdrɛnna.]
It's very bad.	**Гэта вельмі дрэнна.** [ɦɛta ˈvelʲmi ˈdrɛnna.]
It's disgusting.	**Гэта агідна.** [ɦɛta aˈɦidna.]
I'm happy.	**Я шчаслівы /шчаслівая/.** [ʲa ɕasˈlivi /ɕasˈlivaʲa/.]
I'm content.	**Я задаволены /задаволена/.** [ʲa zadaˈvoleni /zadaˈvolena/.]
I'm in love.	**Я закаханы /закахана/.** [ʲa zakaˈhani /zakaˈhana/.]
I'm calm.	**Я спакойны /спакойна/.** [ʲa spaˈkojni /spaˈkojna/.]
I'm bored.	**Мне сумна.** [mne ˈsumna.]
I'm tired.	**Я стаміўся /стамілася/.** [ʲa staˈmiwsʲa /staˈmilasʲa/.]
I'm sad.	**Мне нудна.** [mne ˈnudna.]
I'm frightened.	**Я напужаны /напужана/.** [ʲa naˈpuʒani /naˈpuʒana/.]
I'm angry.	**Я злуюся.** [ʲa zluˈʉsʲa.]
I'm worried.	**Я хвалююся.** [ʲa hvaˈlʉjusʲa.]
I'm nervous.	**Я нярвуюся.** [ʲa nʲarˈvuʉsʲa.]

I'm jealous. (envious)	**Я зайздрошчу.** [ˈa zajzdˈroɕu.]
I'm surprised.	**Я здзіўлены /здзіўлена/.** [ˈa ˈzdʑiwleni /ˈzdʑiwlena/.]
I'm perplexed.	**Я азадачаны /азадачана/.** [ˈa azaˈdatʃani /azaˈdatʃana/.]

Problems. Accidents

I've got a problem.	**У мяне праблема.** [u mʲa'ne prab'lema.]
We've got a problem.	**У нас праблема.** [u nas prab'lema.]
I'm lost.	**Я заблукаў /заблукала/.** [ʲa zablu'kaw /zablu'kala/.]
I missed the last bus (train).	**Я спазніўся на апошні аўтобус (цягнік).** [ʲa spaz'niwsʲa na a'poʃni aw'tɔbus (tsʲaɦ'nik).]
I don't have any money left.	**У мяне зусім не засталося грошай.** [u mʲa'ne zu'sim ne zasta'lɔsʲa 'ɦrɔʃaj.]

I've lost my …	**Я згубіў /згубіла/…** [ʲa zɦu'biw /zɦu'bila/ …]
Someone stole my …	**У мяне ўкралі …** [u mʲa'ne w'krali …]

passport	**пашпарт** [paʃpart]
wallet	**кашалёк** [kaʃa'lʲok]
papers	**дакументы** [daku'mentɨ]
ticket	**білет** [bi'let]

money	**грошы** [ɦrɔʃɨ]
handbag	**сумку** [sumku]
camera	**фотаапарат** [fɔtaapa'rat]
laptop	**ноутбук** [nɔut'buk]
tablet computer	**планшэт** [plan'ʃɛt]
mobile phone	**тэлефон** [tɛle'fɔn]

Help me!	**Дапамажыце!** [dapama'ʒɨtse]
What's happened?	**Што здарылася?** [ʃtɔ 'zdarɨlasʲa?]

fire	пажар
	[pa'ʒar]
shooting	стралянiна
	[stralʲa'nina]
murder	забойства
	[za'bɔjstva]
explosion	выбух
	[vɨbuh]
fight	бойка
	[bɔjka]

Call the police!	Выклiкайце мiлiцыю!
	[vɨklikajtse mi'litsɨʉ!]
Please hurry up!	Калi ласка, хутчэй!
	[ka'li 'laska, huʧɛjʲ!]
I'm looking for the police station.	Я шукаю аддзяленне мiлiцыi.
	[ʲa ʃu'kaʉ adzʲa'lenne mi'litsɨi.]
I need to make a call.	Мне трэба пазванiць.
	[mne 'trɛba pazva'nitsʲ.]
May I use your phone?	Магу я пазванiць?
	[ma'hu ʲa pazva'nitsʲ?]

I've been ...	Мяне ...
	[mʲa'ne ...]
mugged	абрабавалi
	[abraba'vali]
robbed	абкралi
	[ab'krali]
raped	згвалтавалi
	[zɦvalta'vali]
attacked (beaten up)	збiлi
	[zbili]

Are you all right?	З вамi ўсё ў парадку?
	[z 'vami wsʲo w pa'ratku?]
Did you see who it was?	Вы бачылi, хто гэта быў?
	[vɨ 'baʧɨli, htɔ 'ɦɛta bɨw?]
Would you be able to recognize the person?	Вы зможаце яго пазнаць?
	[vɨ 'zmɔʒatse ʲa'ɦɔ paz'natsʲ?]
Are you sure?	Вы дакладна ўпэўнены?
	[vɨ dak'ladna u'pɛwneni?]

Please calm down.	Калi ласка, супакойцеся.
	[ka'li 'laska, supa'kɔjtsesʲa.]
Take it easy!	Спакайней!
	[spakaj'nej!]
Don't worry!	Не турбуйцеся.
	[ne tur'bujtsesʲa.]
Everything will be fine.	Усё будзе добра.
	[wsʲo 'budze 'dɔbra.]
Everything's all right.	Усё ў парадку.
	[wsʲo w pa'ratku.]

Come here, please.	**Падыдзіце, калі ласка.** [padi'dzitse, ka'li 'laska.]
I have some questions for you.	**У мяне да вас некалькі пытанняў.** [u mⁱa'ne da vas 'nekalⁱki pi'tannⁱaw.]
Wait a moment, please.	**Пачакайце, калі ласка.** [patʃa'kajtse, ka'li 'laska.]
Do you have any I.D.?	**У вас ёсць дакументы?** [u vas ⁱostsⁱ daku'menti?]
Thanks. You can leave now.	**Дзякуй. Вы можаце ісці.** [dzⁱakuj. vⁱ mɔʒatse isⁱtsi.]
Hands behind your head!	**Рукі за галаву!** [ruki za ɦala'vu!]
You're under arrest!	**Вы арыштаваны.** [vⁱ ariʃta'vani!]

Health problems

Please help me.	**Дапамажыце, калі ласка.** [dapama'ʒɨtse, ka'li 'laska.]
I don't feel well.	**Мне дрэнна.** [mne 'drɛnna.]
My husband doesn't feel well.	**Майму мужу дрэнна.** [majmu 'muʒu 'drɛnna.]
My son ...	**Майму сыну ...** [majmu 'sɨnu ...]
My father ...	**Майму бацьку ...** [majmu 'batsʲku ...]
My wife doesn't feel well.	**Маёй жонцы дрэнна.** [ma'oj 'ʒɔntsɨ 'drɛnna.]
My daughter ...	**Маёй дачцэ ...** [ma'oj datʃ'tsɛ ...]
My mother ...	**Маёй маці ...** [ma'oj 'matsi ...]
I've got a ...	**У мяне баліць ...** [u mʲa'ne ba'litsʲ ...]
headache	**галава** [ħala'va]
sore throat	**горла** [ħɔrla]
stomach ache	**жывот** [ʒɨ'vɔt]
toothache	**зуб** [zub]
I feel dizzy.	**У мяне кружыцца галава.** [u mʲa'ne 'kruʒɨtsa ħala'va.]
He has a fever.	**У яго тэмпература.** [u ʲa'ħɔ tɛmpera'tura.]
She has a fever.	**У яе тэмпература.** [u ʲae tɛmpera'tura.]
I can't breathe.	**Я не магу дыхаць.** [ʲa ne ma'ħu 'dɨhatsʲ.]
I'm short of breath.	**Я задыхаюся.** [ʲa zadɨ'hausʲa.]
I am asthmatic.	**Я астматык.** [ʲa ast'matɨk.]
I am diabetic.	**Я дыябетык.** [ʲa dʲʲa'betɨk.]

I can't sleep.	**У мяне бяссонніца.** [u mʲaˈne bʲasˈsɔnnitsa.]
food poisoning	**харчовае атручванне** [harˈtʃovae atˈrutʃvanne]

It hurts here.	**Баліць вось тут.** [baˈlitsʲ vɔsʲ tut.]
Help me!	**Дапамажыце!** [dapamaˈʒitse!]
I am here!	**Я тут!** [ˈʲa tut!]
We are here!	**Мы тут!** [mɨ tut!]
Get me out of here!	**Выцягніце мяне!** [vitsʲaɦnitse mʲaˈne!]
I need a doctor.	**Мне патрэбны доктар.** [mne paˈtrɛbnɨ ˈdɔktar.]
I can't move.	**Я не магу рухацца.** [ˈʲa ne maˈɦu ˈruhatsa.]
I can't move my legs.	**Я не адчуваю ног.** [ˈʲa ne attʃuˈvaʉ nɔɦ.]

I have a wound.	**Я паранены /паранена/.** [ˈʲa paˈranenɨ /paˈranena/.]
Is it serious?	**Гэта сур'ёзна?** [ɦɛta suˈrʲʲozna?]
My documents are in my pocket.	**Мае дакументы ў кішэні.** [maˈe dakuˈmentɨ w kiˈʃɛni.]
Calm down!	**Супакойцеся!** [supaˈkɔjtsesʲaǃ]
May I use your phone?	**Магу я пазваніць?** [maˈɦu ˈʲa pazvaˈnitsʲ?]

Call an ambulance!	**Выклікайце хуткую падамогу!** [viklikajtse ˈhutkuʉ padaˈmɔɦuǃ]
It's urgent!	**Гэта неадкладна!** [ɦɛta neatˈkladnaǃ]
It's an emergency!	**Гэта вельмі неадкладна!** [ɦɛta ˈvelʲmi neatˈkladnaǃ]
Please hurry up!	**Калі ласка, хутчэй!** [kaˈli ˈlaska, huˈtʃɛjǃ]
Would you please call a doctor?	**Выклікайце доктара, калі ласка!** [viklikajtse ˈdɔktara, kaˈli ˈlaskaǃ]
Where is the hospital?	**Скажыце, дзе бальніца?** [skaˈʒitse, dze balʲˈnitsa?]

How are you feeling?	**Як вы сябе адчуваеце?** [ˈʲak vɨ sʲaˈbe attʃuˈvaetse?]
Are you all right?	**З вамі ўсё ў парадку?** [z ˈvami wsʲo w paˈratku?]
What's happened?	**Что здарылася?** [tʃtɔ ˈzdarilasʲa?]

I feel better now.

Мне ўжо лепш.
[mne wʒɔ lepʃ.]

It's OK.

Ўсё ў парадку.
[wsʲo w pa'ratku.]

It's all right.

Усё добра.
[wsʲo 'dɔbra.]

At the pharmacy

pharmacy (drugstore)	**аптэка** [ap'tɛka]
24-hour pharmacy	**кругласутачная аптэка** [kruɦla'sutatʃnaʲa ap'tɛka]
Where is the closest pharmacy?	**Дзе бліжэйшая аптэка?** [dze bli'ʒɛjʃaʲa ap'tɛka?]
Is it open now?	**Яна зараз адчынена?** [ʲa'na 'zaraz at'tʃɨnena?]
At what time does it open?	**А якой гадзіне яна адчыняецца?** [a ʲakɔj ɦa'dzine ʲana attʃi'nʲaetsa?]
At what time does it close?	**Да якой гадзіны яна працуе?** [da ʲa'kɔj ɦa'dzinɨ ʲa'na pra'tsue?]
Is it far?	**Гэта далёка?** [ɦɛta da'lʲoka?]
Can I get there on foot?	**Я дайду туды пешшу?** [ʲa daj'du tu'dɨ 'peʃu?]
Can you show me on the map?	**Пакажыце мне на карце, калі ласка.** [paka'ʒɨtse mne na kartse, ka'li 'laska.]
Please give me something for ...	**Дайце мне чаго-небудзь ад ...** [dajtse mne tʃaɦɔ 'nebutsʲ at ...]
a headache	**галаўнога болю** [ɦalaw'nɔɦa 'bolʉ]
a cough	**кашлю** [kaʃlʉ]
a cold	**прастуды** [pra'studɨ]
the flu	**грыпу** [ɦrɨpu]
a fever	**тэмпературы** [tɛmpera'turɨ]
a stomach ache	**болю ў страўніку** [bolʉ w 'strawniku]
nausea	**млоснасці** [mlɔsnasʲtsi]
diarrhea	**дыярэі** [dʲʲa'rɛi]
constipation	**запору** [za'pɔru]
pain in the back	**боль у спіне** [bolʲ u spine]

chest pain	**боль у грудзях** [bɔlʲ u ɦru'dzʲah]
side stitch	**боль у баку** [bɔlʲ u ba'ku]
abdominal pain	**боль у жываце** [bɔlʲ u ʒɨvatse]
pill	**таблетка** [tab'letka]
ointment, cream	**мазь, крэм** [mazʲ, krɛm]
syrup	**сіроп** [si'rɔp]
spray	**спрэй** [sprɛj]
drops	**кроплі** [krɔpli]
You need to go to the hospital.	**Вам патрэбна ў бальніцу.** [vam pa'trɛbna w balʲnitsu.]
health insurance	**страхоўка** [stra'hɔwka]
prescription	**рэцэпт** [rɛ'tsɛpt]
insect repellant	**сродак ад насякомых** [srɔdak ad nasʲa'kɔmih]
Band Aid	**лейкапластыр** [lejka'plastɨr]

The bare minimum

Excuse me, ...	**Прабачце, ...** [pra'batʃtse, ...]
Hello.	**Прывітанне.** [privi'tanne.]
Thank you.	**Дзякуй.** [dzʲakuj.]
Good bye.	**Да пабачэння.** [da paba'tʃɛnnʲa.]
Yes.	**Так.** [tak.]
No.	**Не.** [ne.]
I don't know.	**Я ня ведаю.** [ʲa nʲa 'vedaʉ.]
Where? | Where to? | When?	**Дзе? | Куды? | Калі?** [dze? | ku'di? | ka'li?]

I need ...	**Мне трэба ...** [mne 'trɛba ...]
I want ...	**Я хачу ...** [ʲa ha'tʃu ...]
Do you have ...?	**У вас ёсць ...?** [u vas ʲostsʲ ...?]
Is there a ... here?	**Тут ёсць ...?** [tut ʲostsʲ ...?]
May I ...?	**Я магу ...?** [ʲa ma'hu ...?]
..., please (polite request)	**Калі ласка** [ka'li 'laska]

I'm looking for ...	**Я шукаю ...** [ʲa ʃu'kaʉ ...]
restroom	**туалет** [tua'let]
ATM	**банкамат** [banka'mat]
pharmacy (drugstore)	**аптэку** [ap'tɛku]
hospital	**бальніцу** [balj'nitsu]
police station	**аддзяленне міліцыі** [adzʲa'lenne mi'litsii]
subway	**метро** [me'trɔ]

taxi	**таксі** [tak'si]
train station	**вакзал** [vak'zal]

My name is …	**Мяне завуць …** [mʲaˈne zaˈvutsʲ …]
What's your name?	**Як вас завуць?** [ˈjak vas zaˈvutsʲ?]
Could you please help me?	**Дапамажыце мне, калі ласка.** [dapamaˈʒɨtse mne, kaˈli ˈlaska?]
I've got a problem.	**У мяне праблема.** [u mʲaˈne prabˈlema.]
I don't feel well.	**Мне дрэнна.** [mne ˈdrɛnna.]
Call an ambulance!	**Выклікайце хуткую дапамогу!** [vɨklikajtse ˈhutkuʉ dapaˈmɔɦu!]
May I make a call?	**Магу я пазваніць?** [maˈɦu ʲa pazvaˈnitsʲ?]

I'm sorry.	**Выбачце.** [vɨbatʃtse.]
You're welcome.	**Калі ласка.** [kaˈli ˈlaska.]

I, me	**я** [ˈja]
you (inform.)	**ты** [tɨ]
he	**ён** [ˈjon]
she	**яна** [ˈjaˈna]
they (masc.)	**яны** [ˈjaˈnɨ]
they (fem.)	**яны** [ˈjaˈnɨ]
we	**мы** [mɨ]
you (pl)	**вы** [vɨ]
you (sg, form.)	**вы** [vɨ]

ENTRANCE	**УВАХОД** [uvaˈhɔd]
EXIT	**ВЫХАД** [vɨhad]
OUT OF ORDER	**НЕ ПРАЦУЕ** [ne praˈtsue]
CLOSED	**ЗАЧЫНЕНА** [zaˈtʃɨnena]

OPEN	**АДЧЫНЕНА** [at'tʃinena]
FOR WOMEN	**ДЛЯ ЖАНЧЫН** [dlʲa ʒan'tʃin]
FOR MEN	**ДЛЯ МУЖЧЫН** [dlʲa muʒ'tʃin]

T&P BOOKS

CONCISE DICTIONARY

This section contains more than 1,500 useful words arranged alphabetically. The dictionary includes a lot of gastronomic terms and will be helpful when ordering food at a restaurant or buying groceries

T&P Books Publishing

DICTIONARY CONTENTS

T&P Books Publishing

time	час (м)	['ʧas]
hour	гадзіна (ж)	[ɦaˈdzina]
half an hour	паўгадзіны	[pawɦaˈdzini]
minute	хвіліна (ж)	[hviˈlina]
second	секунда (ж)	[seˈkunda]

today (adv)	сёння	[ˈsʲɔnnʲa]
tomorrow (adv)	заўтра	[ˈzawtra]
yesterday (adv)	учора	[uˈʧɔra]

Monday	панядзелак (м)	[panʲaˈdzelak]
Tuesday	аўторак (м)	[awˈtɔrak]
Wednesday	серада (ж)	[seraˈda]
Thursday	чацвер (м)	[ʧaʦˈver]
Friday	пятніца (ж)	[ˈpʲatnitsa]
Saturday	субота (ж)	[suˈbɔta]
Sunday	нядзеля (ж)	[nʲaˈdzelʲa]

day	дзень (м)	[ˈdzenʲ]
working day	працоўны дзень (м)	[praˈtsɔwni ˈdzenʲ]
public holiday	святочны дзень (м)	[svʲaˈtɔʧnʲi ˈdzenʲ]
weekend	выхадныя (м мн)	[viɦadˈnʲʲa]

week	тыдзень (м)	[ˈtidzenʲ]
last week (adv)	на мінулым тыдні	[na miˈnulim ˈtidni]
next week (adv)	на наступным тыдні	[na naˈstupnim ˈtidni]

sunrise	узыход (м) сонца	[uziˈɦɔt ˈsɔnʦa]
sunset	захад (м)	[ˈzaɦat]

in the morning	ранкам	[ˈrankam]
in the afternoon	пасля абеду	[paˈslʲa aˈbedu]

in the evening	увечар	[uˈveʧar]
tonight (this evening)	сёння ўвечары	[sʲonnʲa uˈweʧari]

at night	уначы	[unaˈʧɨ]
midnight	поўнач (ж)	[ˈpɔwnaʧ]

January	студзень (м)	[ˈstudzenʲ]
February	люты (м)	[ˈlʉti]
March	сакавік (м)	[sakaˈvik]
April	красавік (м)	[krasaˈvik]
May	май (м)	[ˈmaj]
June	чэрвень (м)	[ˈʧɛrvenʲ]

July	ліпень (м)	['lipenʲ]
August	жнівень (м)	['ʒnivenʲ]
September	верасень (м)	['verasenʲ]
October	кастрычнік (м)	[kas'tritʃnik]
November	лістапад (м)	[lista'pat]
December	снежань (м)	['sneʒanʲ]

in spring	увесну	[u'vesnu]
in summer	улетку	[u'letku]
in fall	увосень	[u'vɔsenʲ]
in winter	узімку	[u'zimku]

month	месяц (м)	['mesʲats]
season (summer, etc.)	сезон (м)	[se'zɔn]
year	год (м)	['hɔt]
century	стагоддзе (н)	[sta'hɔdze]

2. Numbers. Numerals

digit, figure	лічба (ж)	['lidʒba]
number	лік (м)	['lik]
minus sign	мінус (м)	['minus]
plus sign	плюс (м)	['plʉs]
sum, total	сума (ж)	['suma]

first (adj)	першы	['perʃɨ]
second (adj)	другі	[dru'hi]
third (adj)	трэці	['trɛtsi]

0 zero	нуль (м)	['nulʲ]
1 one	адзін	[a'dzin]
2 two	два	['dva]
3 three	тры	['trɨ]
4 four	чатыры	[tʃa'tɨrɨ]

5 five	пяць	['pʲatsʲ]
6 six	шэсць	['ʃɛstsʲ]
7 seven	сем	['sem]
8 eight	восем	['vɔsem]
9 nine	дзевяць	['dzevʲatsʲ]
10 ten	дзесяць	['dzesʲatsʲ]

11 eleven	адзінаццаць	[adzi'natsatsʲ]
12 twelve	дванаццаць	[dva'natsatsʲ]
13 thirteen	трынаццаць	[trɨ'natsatsʲ]
14 fourteen	чатырнаццаць	[tʃatɨr'natsatsʲ]
15 fifteen	пятнаццаць	[pʲat'natsatsʲ]

| 16 sixteen | шаснаццаць | [ʃas'natsatsʲ] |
| 17 seventeen | семнаццаць | [sʲam'natsatsʲ] |

| 18 eighteen | васемнаццаць | [vasʲam'natsatsʲ] |
| 19 nineteen | дзевятнаццаць | [dzevʲat'natsatsʲ] |

20 twenty	дваццаць	['dvatsatsʲ]
30 thirty	трыццаць	['tritsatsʲ]
40 forty	сорак	['sɔrak]
50 fifty	пяцьдзесят	[pʲadzʲa'sʲat]

60 sixty	шэсцьдзесят	['ʃɛzʲdzesʲat]
70 seventy	семдзесят	['semdzesʲat]
80 eighty	восемдзесят	['vɔsemdzesʲat]
90 ninety	дзевяноста	[dzevʲa'nɔsta]

100 one hundred	сто	['stɔ]
200 two hundred	дзвесце	[dzj'vesʲtse]
300 three hundred	трыста	['trista]
400 four hundred	чатырыста	[ʧa'tirista]
500 five hundred	пяцьсот	[pʲatsʲ'sɔt]

600 six hundred	шэсцьсот	[ʃɛstsʲ'sɔt]
700 seven hundred	семсот	[sem'sɔt]
800 eight hundred	восемсот	[vɔsem'sɔt]
900 nine hundred	дзевяцьсот	[dzevʲatsʲ'sɔt]
1000 one thousand	тысяча	['tisʲaʧa]

| 10000 ten thousand | дзесяць тысяч | ['dzesʲatsʲ 'tisʲaʧ] |
| one hundred thousand | сто тысяч | ['stɔ 'tisʲaʧ] |

| million | мільён (м) | [mi'ljɔn] |
| billion | мільярд (м) | [mi'lʲart] |

3. Humans. Family

man (adult male)	мужчына (м)	[mu'ʃɕina]
young man	юнак (м)	[ʉ'nak]
teenager	падлетак (м)	[pad'letak]
woman	жанчына (ж)	[ʒan'ʧina]
girl (young woman)	дзяўчына (ж)	[dzʲaw'ʧina]

age	узрост (м)	[uz'rɔst]
adult (adj)	дарослы	[da'rɔslɨ]
middle-aged (adj)	сярэдніх гадоў	[sʲa'rɛdnih ha'dɔw]
elderly (adj)	пажылы	[paʒɨ'lʲi]
old (adj)	стары	[sta'rɨ]

old man	стары (м)	[sta'ri]
old woman	старая (ж)	[sta'raʲa]
retirement	пенсія (ж)	['pensiʲa]
to retire (from job)	пайсці на пенсію	[pajsʲ'tsi na 'pensiʉ]
retiree	пенсіянер (м)	[pensiʲa'ner]

mother	маці (ж)	['matsi]
father	бацька (м)	['batsʲka]
son	сын (м)	['sin]
daughter	дачка (ж)	[datʃʼka]
brother	брат (м)	['brat]
elder brother	старшы брат (м)	['starʃi 'brat]
younger brother	меншы брат (м)	['menʃi 'brat]
sister	сястра (ж)	[sʲast'ra]
elder sister	старшая сястра (ж)	['starʃaʲa sʲas'tra]
younger sister	малодшая сястра (ж)	[ma'lɔtʃaʲa sʲas'tra]
parents	бацькі (мн)	[batsʲʼki]
child	дзіця (н)	[dzi'tsʲa]
children	дзеці (н мн)	['dzetsi]
stepmother	мачаха (ж)	['matʃaha]
stepfather	айчым (м)	[aj'tʃim]
grandmother	бабуля (ж)	[ba'bulʲa]
grandfather	дзядуля (м)	[dzʲa'dulʲa]
grandson	унук (м)	[u'nuk]
granddaughter	унучка (ж)	[u'nutʃka]
grandchildren	унукі (м мн)	[u'nuki]
uncle	дзядзька (м)	['dzʲatsʲka]
aunt	цётка (ж)	['tsʲotka]
nephew	пляменнік (м)	[plʲa'mennik]
niece	пляменніца (ж)	[plʲa'mennitsa]
wife	жонка (ж)	['ʒɔnka]
husband	муж (м)	['muʃ]
married (masc.)	жанаты	[ʒa'nati]
married (fem.)	замужняя	[za'muʒnæʲa]
widow	удава (ж)	[u'dava]
widower	удавец (м)	[uda'vets]
name (first name)	імя (н)	[i'mʲa]
surname (last name)	прозвішча (н)	['prɔzʲviʃɕa]
relative	свaяк (м)	[sva'ʲak]
friend (masc.)	сябар (м)	['sʲabar]
friendship	сяброўства (н)	[sʲab'rɔwstva]
partner	партнёр (м)	[part'nʲor]
superior (n)	начальнік (м)	[na'tʃalʲnik]
colleague	калега (м, ж)	[ka'leɦa]
neighbors	суседзі (м мн)	[su'sedzi]

4. Human body

organism (body)	арганізм (м)	[arɦa'nizm]
body	цела (н)	['tsela]

heart	сэрца (н)	['sɛrtsa]
blood	кроў (ж)	['krɔw]
brain	мозг (м)	['mɔsk]
nerve	нерв (м)	['nerv]

bone	косць (ж)	['kɔstsʲ]
skeleton	шкілет (м)	[ʃki'let]
spine (backbone)	пазваночнік (м)	[pazva'nɔtʃnik]
rib	рабро (н)	[rab'rɔ]
skull	чэрап (м)	['tʃɛrap]

muscle	цягліца (ж)	[tsʲah'litsa]
lungs	лёгкія (н мн)	['lʲoɦkiʲa]
skin	скура (ж)	['skura]

head	галава (ж)	[ɦala'va]
face	твар (м)	['tvar]
nose	нос (м)	['nɔs]
forehead	лоб (м)	['lɔp]
cheek	шчака (ж)	[ʃɕa'ka]

mouth	рот (м)	['rɔt]
tongue	язык (м)	[ʲa'zɨk]
tooth	зуб (м)	['zup]
lips	губы (ж мн)	['ɦubɨ]
chin	падбародак (м)	[padba'rɔdak]

ear	вуха (н)	['vuɦa]
neck	шыя (ж)	['ʃɨʲa]
throat	горла (н)	['ɦɔrla]

eye	вока (н)	['vɔka]
pupil	зрэнка (ж)	['zrɛnka]
eyebrow	брыво (н)	[brɨ'vɔ]
eyelash	вейка (ж)	['vejka]

hair	валасы (м мн)	[vala'sɨ]
hairstyle	прычоска (ж)	[prɨ'tʃɔska]
mustache	вусы (м мн)	['vusɨ]
beard	барада (ж)	[bara'da]
to have (a beard, etc.)	насіць	[na'sitsʲ]
bald (adj)	лысы	['lɨsɨ]

hand	кісць (ж)	['kistsʲ]
arm	рука (ж)	[ru'ka]
finger	палец (м)	['palets]
nail	пазногаць (м)	[paz'nɔɦatsʲ]
palm	далонь (ж)	[da'lɔnʲ]

shoulder	плячо (н)	[plʲa'tʃɔ]
leg	нага (ж)	[na'ɦa]
foot	ступня (ж)	[stup'nʲa]

| knee | калена (н) | [ka'lena] |
| heel | пятка (ж) | ['pʲatka] |

back	спіна (ж)	['spina]
waist	талія (ж)	['taliʲa]
beauty mark	радзімка (ж)	[ra'dzimka]
birthmark (café au lait spot)	радзімая пляма (ж)	[ra'dzimaʲa 'plʲama]

5. Medicine. Diseases. Drugs

health	здароўе (н)	[zda'rɔwe]
well (not sick)	здаровы	[zda'rɔvi]
sickness	хвароба (ж)	[hva'rɔba]
to be sick	хварэць	[hva'rɛtsʲ]
ill, sick (adj)	хворы	['hvɔri]

cold (illness)	прастуда (ж)	[pra'studa]
to catch a cold	прастудзіцца	[prastu'dzitsa]
tonsillitis	ангіна (ж)	[an'hina]
pneumonia	запаленне (н) лёгкіх	[zapa'lenne 'lʲohkih]
flu, influenza	грып (м)	['hrip]

runny nose (coryza)	насмарк (м)	['nasmark]
cough	кашаль (м)	['kaʃalʲ]
to cough (vi)	кашляць	['kaʃlʲatsʲ]
to sneeze (vi)	чхаць	['tʃhatsʲ]

stroke	інсульт (м)	[in'sulʲt]
heart attack	інфаркт (м)	[in'farkt]
allergy	алергія (ж)	[aler'hiʲa]
asthma	астма (ж)	['astma]
diabetes	дыябет (м)	[dʲa'bet]

tumor	пухліна (ж)	[puh'lina]
cancer	рак (м)	['rak]
alcoholism	алкагалізм (м)	[alkaha'lizm]
AIDS	СНІД (м)	['snit]
fever	ліхаманка (ж)	[liha'manka]
seasickness	марская хвароба (ж)	[mar'skaʲa hva'rɔba]

bruise (hématome)	сіняк (м)	[si'nʲak]
bump (lump)	гуз (м)	['hus]
to limp (vi)	кульгаць	[kulʲ'hatsʲ]
dislocation	звіх (м)	['zʲvih]
to dislocate (vt)	звіхнуць	[zʲvih'nutsʲ]

fracture	пералом (м)	[pera'lɔm]
burn (injury)	апёк (м)	[a'pʲok]
injury	пашкоджанне (н)	[paʃ'kɔdʒanne]

| pain, ache | боль (м) | ['bɔlʲ] |
| toothache | зубны боль (м) | [zubˈnɨ 'bɔlʲ] |

to sweat (perspire)	пацець	[paˈtsetsʲ]
deaf (adj)	глухі	[ɣluˈhi]
mute (adj)	нямы	[nʲaˈmɨ]

immunity	імунітэт (м)	[imuniˈtɛt]
virus	вірус (м)	['virus]
microbe	мікроб (м)	[mikˈrɔp]
bacterium	бактэрыя (ж)	[bakˈtɛrɨʲa]
infection	інфекцыя (ж)	[inˈfektsɨʲa]

hospital	бальніца (ж)	[balʲˈnitsa]
cure	лячэнне (н)	[lʲaˈtʃɛnne]
to vaccinate (vt)	рабіць прышчэпку	[raˈbitsʲ prɨˈʃɕɛpku]
to be in a coma	быць у коме	[bɨtsʲ u ˈkɔme]
intensive care	рэанімацыя (ж)	[rɛaniˈmatsɨʲa]
symptom	сімптом (м)	[simpˈtɔm]
pulse	пульс (м)	['pulʲs]

6. Feelings. Emotions. Conversation

I, me	я	[ʲa]
you	ты	[tɨ]
he	ён	[ʲon]
she	яна	[ʲaˈna]
it	яно	[ʲaˈnɔ]

we	мы	['mɨ]
you (to a group)	вы	['vɨ]
they	яны	[ʲaˈnɨ]

Hello! (fam.)	Вітаю!	[viˈtau]
Hello! (form.)	Вітаю вас!	[viˈtau vas]
Good morning!	Добрай раніцы!	[dobraj ˈranitsɨ]
Good afternoon!	Добры дзень!	[dobrɨ 'dzenʲ]
Good evening!	Добры вечар!	[dobrɨ 'vetʃar]

to say hello	вітацца	[viˈtatsa]
to greet (vt)	вітаць	[viˈtatsʲ]
How are you?	Як маецеся?	[ʲak 'maetsesʲa]
Bye-Bye! Goodbye!	Да пабачэння!	[da pabaˈtʃɛnnʲa]
Goodbye! (form.)	Да пабачэння!	[da pabaˈtʃɛnnʲa]
Bye! (fam.)	Бывай!	[bɨˈvaj]
Thank you!	Дзякуй!	['dzʲakuj]

feelings	пачуцці (н мн)	[paˈtʃutsi]
to be hungry	хацець есці	[haˈtsetsʲ 'esʲtsi]
to be thirsty	хацець піць	[haˈtsetsʲ 'pitsʲ]

tired (adj)	стомлены	['stɔmlenɨ]
to be worried	непакоіцца	[nepa'kɔitsa]
to be nervous	нервавацца	[nerva'vatsa]
hope	надзея (ж)	[na'dzeʲa]
to hope (vi, vt)	спадзявацца	[spadzʲa'vatsa]
character	характар (м)	[ha'raktar]
modest (adj)	сціплы	['sʲtsiplɨ]
lazy (adj)	гультаяваты	[ɦulʲtaʲa'vatɨ]
generous (adj)	шчодры	['ʃɕodrɨ]
talented (adj)	таленавіты	[talena'vitɨ]
honest (adj)	сумленны	[sum'lennɨ]
serious (adj)	сур'ёзны	[su'rʲⁱoz'nɨ]
shy, timid (adj)	нясмелы	[nʲa'smelɨ]
sincere (adj)	чыстасардэчны	[tʃistasar'dɛtʃnɨ]
coward	баязлівец (м)	[baʲaz'livets]
to sleep (vi)	спаць	['spatsʲ]
dream	сон (м)	['sɔn]
bed	ложак (м)	['lɔʒak]
pillow	падушка (ж)	[pa'duʃka]
insomnia	бяссонніца (ж)	[bʲas'sɔnnitsa]
to go to bed	ісці спаць	[is'tsi 'spatsʲ]
nightmare	кашмар (м)	[kaʃ'mar]
alarm clock	будзільнік (м)	[bu'dzilʲnik]
smile	усмешка (ж)	[us'meʃka]
to smile (vi)	усміхацца	[usmi'hatsa]
to laugh (vi)	смяяцца	[smæ'ʲʲatsa]
quarrel	сварка (ж)	['svarka]
insult	абраза (ж)	[ab'raza]
resentment	крыўда (ж)	['krɨwda]
angry (mad)	злосны	['zlɔsnɨ]

7. Clothing. Personal accessories

clothes	адзенне (н)	[a'dzenne]
coat (overcoat)	паліто (н)	[pali'tɔ]
fur coat	футра (н)	['futra]
jacket (e.g., leather ~)	куртка (ж)	['kurtka]
raincoat (trenchcoat, etc.)	плашч (м)	['plaʃɕ]
shirt (button shirt)	кашуля (ж)	[ka'ʃulʲa]
pants	штаны (мн)	[ʃta'nɨ]
suit jacket	пінжак (м)	[pin'ʒak]
suit	касцюм (м)	[kas'tsʉm]
dress (frock)	сукенка (ж)	[su'kenka]

skirt	спадніца (ж)	[spad'nitsa]
T-shirt	футболка (ж)	[fud'bɔlka]
bathrobe	халат (м)	[ha'lat]
pajamas	піжама (ж)	[pi'ʒama]
workwear	працоўнае адзенне (н)	[pra'tsɔwnae a'dzenne]

underwear	бялізна (ж)	[bʲa'lizna]
socks	шкарпэткі (ж мн)	[ʃkar'pɛtki]
bra	бюстгальтар (м)	[bʉz'halʲtar]
pantyhose	калготкі (мн)	[kal'hɔtki]
stockings (thigh highs)	панчохі (ж мн)	[pan'tʃɔhi]
bathing suit	купальнік (м)	[ku'palʲnik]

hat	шапка (ж)	['ʃapka]
footwear	абутак (м)	[a'butak]
boots (e.g., cowboy ~)	боты (м мн)	['bɔti]
heel	абцас (м)	[ap'tsas]

| shoestring | шнурок (м) | [ʃnu'rɔk] |
| shoe polish | крэм (м) для абутку | ['krɛm dlʲa a'butku] |

cotton (n)	бавоўна (ж)	[ba'vɔwna]
wool (n)	шэрсць (ж)	['ʃɛrstsʲ]
fur (n)	футра (н)	['futra]

gloves	пальчаткі (ж мн)	[palʲ'tʃatki]
mittens	рукавіцы (ж мн)	[ruka'vitsi]
scarf (muffler)	шалік (м)	['ʃalik]

| glasses (eyeglasses) | акуляры (мн) | [aku'lʲari] |
| umbrella | парасон (м) | [para'sɔn] |

| tie (necktie) | гальштук (м) | ['halʲʃtuk] |
| handkerchief | насоўка (ж) | [na'sɔwka] |

| comb | грабянец (м) | [hrabʲa'nets] |
| hairbrush | шчотка (ж) для валасоў | ['ʃɕɔtka dlʲa vala'sɔw] |

buckle	спражка (ж)	['spraʃka]
belt	пояс (м)	['pɔʲas]
purse	сумачка (ж)	['sumatʃka]

| collar | каўнер (м) | [kaw'ner] |
| pocket | кішэня (ж) | [ki'ʃɛnʲa] |

| sleeve | рукаў (м) | [ru'kaw] |
| fly (on trousers) | прарэх (м) | [pra'rɛh] |

zipper (fastener)	маланка (ж)	[ma'lanka]
button	гузік (м)	['huzik]
to get dirty (vi)	запэцкацца	[za'pɛtskatsa]
stain (mark, spot)	пляма (ж)	['plʲama]

8. City. Urban institutions

store	крама (ж)	['krama]
shopping mall	гандлёвы цэнтр (м)	[hand'lʲovɨ 'tsɛntr]
supermarket	супермаркет (м)	[super'market]
shoe store	абутковая крама (ж)	[abut'kovaʲa 'krama]
bookstore	кнігарня (ж)	[kni'harnʲa]

drugstore, pharmacy	аптэка (ж)	[ap'tɛka]
bakery	булачная (ж)	['bulatʃnaʲa]
pastry shop	кандытарская (ж)	[kan'ditarskaʲa]
grocery store	бакалея (ж)	[baka'leʲa]
butcher shop	мясная крама (ж)	[mʲas'naʲa 'krama]
produce store	крама (ж) гароднiны	['krama ha'rɔdninɨ]
market	рынак (м)	['rɨnak]

hair salon	цырульня (ж)	[tsɨ'rulʲnʲa]
post office	пошта (ж)	['pɔʃta]
dry cleaners	хімчыстка (ж)	[him'tʃistka]
circus	цырк (м)	['tsɨrk]
zoo	заапарк (м)	[zaa'park]

theater	тэатр (м)	[tɛ'atr]
movie theater	кінатэатр (м)	[kinatɛ'atr]
museum	музей (м)	[mu'zej]
library	бібліятэка (ж)	[bibliʲa'tɛka]

mosque	мячэць (ж)	[mʲa'tʃɛtsʲ]
synagogue	сінагога (ж)	[sina'hɔha]
cathedral	сабор (м)	[sa'bɔr]
temple	храм (м)	['hram]
church	царква (ж)	[tsark'va]

college	інстытут (м)	[insti'tut]
university	універсітэт (м)	[universi'tɛt]
school	школа (ж)	['ʃkɔla]

hotel	гасцініца (ж)	[has'tsinitsa]
bank	банк (м)	['bank]
embassy	пасольства (н)	[pa'sɔlʲstva]
travel agency	турагенцтва (н)	[tura'hentstva]

subway	метро (н)	[me'trɔ]
hospital	бальніца (ж)	[balʲi'nitsa]
gas station	бензазапраўка (ж)	['benza za'prawka]
parking lot	аўтастаянка (ж)	[awtasta'ʲanka]

ENTRANCE	УВАХОД	[uva'hɔt]
EXIT	ВЫХАД	['vɨhat]
PUSH	АД СЯБЕ	[at sʲa'be]
PULL	НА СЯБЕ	[na sʲa'be]

| OPEN | АДЧЫНЕНА | [a'tʃɨnena] |
| CLOSED | ЗАЧЫНЕНА | [za'tʃɨnena] |

monument	помнік (м)	['pɔmnik]
fortress	крэпасць (ж)	['krɛpasʲsʲ]
palace	палац (м)	[pa'lats]

medieval (adj)	сярэдневяковы	[sʲarɛdnevʲa'kɔvɨ]
ancient (adj)	старадаўні	[stara'dawni]
national (adj)	нацыянальны	[natsɨja'nalʲnɨ]
famous (monument, etc.)	вядомы	[vʲa'dɔmɨ]

9. Money. Finances

money	грошы (мн)	['ɦrɔʃɨ]
coin	манета (ж)	[ma'neta]
dollar	долар (м)	['dɔlar]
euro	еўра (м)	['ewra]

ATM	банкамат (м)	[banka'mat]
currency exchange	абменны пункт (м)	[ab'mennɨ 'punkt]
exchange rate	курс (м)	['kurs]
cash	гатоўка (ж)	[ɦa'tɔwka]

How much?	Колькі?	['kɔlʲki]
to pay (vi, vt)	плаціць	[pla'tsitsʲ]
payment	аплата (ж)	[a'plata]
change (give the ~)	рэшта (ж)	['rɛʃta]

price	цана (ж)	[tsa'na]
discount	скідка (ж)	['skitka]
cheap (adj)	танны	['tannɨ]
expensive (adj)	дарагі	[dara'ɦi]

bank	банк (м)	['bank]
account	рахунак (м)	[ra'ɦunak]
credit card	крэдытная картка (ж)	[krɛ'dɨtnaʲa 'kartka]
check	чэк (м)	['tʃɛk]
to write a check	выпісаць чэк	['vɨpisatsʲ 'tʃɛk]
checkbook	чэкавая кніжка (ж)	['tʃɛkavaʲa 'kniʃka]

debt	доўг (м)	['dɔwɦ]
debtor	даўжнік (м)	[dawʒ'nik]
to lend (money)	даць у доўг	['datsʲ u 'dɔwɦ]
to borrow (vi, vt)	узяць у доўг	[u'zʲatsʲ u 'dɔwɦ]

to rent (~ a tuxedo)	узяць напракат	[u'zʲatsʲ napra'kat]
on credit (adv)	у крэдыт	[u krɛ'dɨt]
wallet	бумажнік (м)	[bu'maʒnik]
safe	сейф (м)	['sejf]

| inheritance | спадчына (ж) | ['spatʃina] |
| fortune (wealth) | маёмасць (ж) | ['maⁱomastsʲ] |

tax	падатак (м)	[pa'datak]
fine	штраф (м)	['ʃtraf]
to fine (vt)	штрафаваць	[ʃtrafa'vatsʲ]

wholesale (adj)	аптовы	[ap'tovɨ]
retail (adj)	рознічны	['rozʲnitʃnɨ]
to insure (vt)	страхаваць	[straha'vatsʲ]
insurance	страхоўка (ж)	[stra'howka]

capital	капітал (м)	[kapi'tal]
turnover	абарот (м)	[aba'rot]
stock (share)	акцыя (ж)	['aktsʲⁱa]
profit	прыбытак (м)	[prɨ'bɨtak]
profitable (adj)	прыбытковы	[prɨbɨt'kovɨ]

crisis	крызіс (м)	['krizis]
bankruptcy	банкруцтва (н)	[bank'rutstva]
to go bankrupt	збанкрутаваць	[zbankruta'vatsʲ]

accountant	бухгалтар (м)	[buh'ɦaltar]
salary	заработная плата (ж)	[zara'botnaⁱa 'plata]
bonus (money)	прэмія (ж)	['prɛmiⁱa]

10. Transportation

bus	аўтобус (м)	[aw'tobus]
streetcar	трамвай (м)	[tram'vaj]
trolley bus	тралейбус (м)	[tra'lejbus]

to go by ...	ехаць на ...	['ehatsʲ na ...]
to get on (~ the bus)	сесці	['sesʲtsi]
to get off ...	сысці з ...	[sɨs'tsi z ...]

stop (e.g., bus ~)	прыпынак (м)	[prɨ'pɨnak]
terminus	канцавы прыпынак (м)	[kantsa'vɨ prɨ'pɨnak]
schedule	расклад (м)	[ras'klat]
ticket	білет (м)	[bi'let]
to be late (for ...)	спазняцца	[spazʲ'nʲatsa]

taxi, cab	таксі (н)	[tak'si]
by taxi	на таксі	[na tak'si]
taxi stand	стаянка (ж) таксі	[sta'ⁱanka tak'si]

traffic	вулічны рух (м)	['vulitʃnɨ 'ruh]
rush hour	час (м) пік	['tʃas 'pik]
to park (vi)	паркавацца	[parka'vatsa]
subway	метро (н)	[me'tro]

station	станцыя (ж)	['stantsʲʲa]
train	цягнік (м)	[tsʲaɦ'nik]
train station	вакзал (м)	[vaɦ'zal]
rails	рэйкі (ж мн)	['rɛjki]
compartment	купэ (н)	[ku'pɛ]
berth	лаўка (ж)	['lawka]

airplane	самалёт (м)	[sama'lʲot]
air ticket	авіябілет (м)	[aviʲabi'let]
airline	авіякампанія (ж)	[aviʲakam'paniʲa]
airport	аэрапорт (м)	[aɛra'pɔrt]

flight (act of flying)	палёт (м)	[pa'lʲot]
luggage	багаж (м)	[ba'ɦaʃ]
luggage cart	каляска (ж) для багажу	[ka'lʲaska dlʲa baɦaʒu]

ship	карабель (м)	[kara'belʲ]
cruise ship	лайнер (м)	['lajner]
yacht	яхта (ж)	['ʲahta]
boat (flat-bottomed ~)	лодка (ж)	['lɔtka]

captain	капітан (м)	[kapi'tan]
cabin	каюта (ж)	[ka'ɵta]
port (harbor)	порт (м)	['pɔrt]

bicycle	веласіпед (м)	[velasi'pet]
scooter	мотаролер (м)	[mɔta'rɔler]
motorcycle, bike	матацыкл (м)	[mata'tsɨkl]
pedal	педаль (ж)	[pe'dalʲ]
pump	помпа (ж)	['pɔmpa]
wheel	кола (н)	['kɔla]

automobile, car	аўтамабіль (м)	[awtama'bilʲ]
ambulance	хуткая дапамога (ж)	[ɦutkaʲa dapa'mɔɦa]
truck	грузавік (м)	[ɦruza'vik]
used (adj)	ужываны	[uʒɨ'vani]
car crash	аварыя (ж)	[a'variʲa]
repair	рамонт (м)	[ra'mɔnt]

11. Food. Part 1

meat	мяса (н)	['mʲasa]
chicken	курыца (ж)	['kuritsa]
duck	качка (ж)	['katʃka]
pork	свініна (ж)	[svi'nina]
veal	цяляціна (ж)	[tsʲa'lʲatsina]
lamb	бараніна (ж)	[ba'ranina]
beef	ялавічына (ж)	['ʲalavitʃina]
sausage (bologna, pepperoni, etc.)	каўбаса (ж)	[kawba'sa]

egg	яйка (н)	['ɨajka]
fish	рыба (ж)	['riba]
cheese	сыр (м)	['sɨr]
sugar	цукар (м)	['tsukar]
salt	соль (ж)	['sɔlɨ]

rice	рыс (м)	['ris]
pasta (macaroni)	макарона (ж)	[maka'rɔna]
butter	масла (н)	['masla]
vegetable oil	алей (м)	[a'lej]
bread	хлеб (м)	['hlep]
chocolate (n)	шакалад (м)	[ʃaka'lat]

wine	віно (н)	[vi'nɔ]
coffee	кава (ж)	['kava]
milk	малако (н)	[mala'kɔ]
juice	сок (м)	['sɔk]

| beer | піва (н) | ['piva] |
| tea | чай (м) | ['tʃaj] |

tomato	памідор (м)	[pami'dɔr]
cucumber	агурок (м)	[aɦu'rɔk]
carrot	морква (ж)	['mɔrkva]
potato	бульба (ж)	['bulɨba]

| onion | цыбуля (ж) | [tsɨ'bulɨa] |
| garlic | часнок (м) | [tʃas'nɔk] |

cabbage	капуста (ж)	[ka'pusta]
beetroot	бурак (м)	[bu'rak]
eggplant	баклажан (м)	[bakla'ʒan]
dill	кроп (м)	['krɔp]

| lettuce | салата (ж) | [sa'lata] |
| corn (maize) | кукуруза (ж) | [kuku'ruza] |

fruit	фрукт (м)	['frukt]
apple	яблык (м)	['ɨablɨk]
pear	груша (ж)	['ɦruʃa]
lemon	лімон (м)	[li'mɔn]

| orange | апельсін (м) | [apelɨ'sin] |
| strawberry (garden ~) | клубніцы (ж мн) | [klub'nitsɨ] |

plum	сліва (ж)	['sliva]
raspberry	маліны (ж мн)	[ma'linɨ]
pineapple	ананас (м)	[ana'nas]
banana	банан (м)	[ba'nan]
watermelon	кавун (м)	[ka'vun]
grape	вінаград (м)	[vina'ɦrat]
melon	дыня (ж)	['dɨnɨa]

12. Food. Part 2

cuisine	кухня (ж)	['kuhnʲa]
recipe	рэцэпт (м)	[rɛ'tsɛpt]
food	ежа (ж)	['eʒa]

to have breakfast	снедаць	['snedatsʲ]
to have lunch	абедаць	[a'bedatsʲ]
to have dinner	вячэраць	[vʲa'tʃɛratsʲ]

taste, flavor	смак (м)	['smak]
tasty (adj)	смачны	['smatʃni]
cold (adj)	халодны	[ha'lɔdni]
hot (adj)	гарачы	[ha'ratʃi]
sweet (sugary)	салодкі	[sa'lɔtki]
salty (adj)	салёны	[sa'lʲoni]

sandwich (bread)	бутэрброд (м)	[butɛr'brɔt]
side dish	гарнір (м)	[har'nir]
filling (for cake, pie)	начынка (ж)	[na'tʃinka]
sauce	соус (м)	['sɔus]
piece (of cake, pie)	кавалак (м)	[ka'valak]

diet	дыета (ж)	[di'eta]
vitamin	вітамін (м)	[vita'min]
calorie	калорыя (ж)	[ka'lɔrʲia]
vegetarian (n)	вегетарыянец (м)	[veɦetari'ʲanets]

restaurant	рэстаран (м)	[rɛsta'ran]
coffee house	кавярня (ж)	[ka'vʲarnʲa]
appetite	апетыт (м)	[ape'tit]
Enjoy your meal!	Смачна есці!	[smatʃna 'esʲtsi]

waiter	афіцыянт (м)	[afitsi'ʲant]
waitress	афіцыянтка (ж)	[afitsi'ʲantka]
bartender	бармэн (м)	[bar'mɛn]
menu	меню (н)	[me'nʉ]

spoon	лыжка (ж)	['liʃka]
knife	нож (м)	['nɔʃ]
fork	відэлец (м)	[vi'dɛlets]
cup (e.g., coffee ~)	кубак (м)	['kubak]

plate (dinner ~)	талерка (ж)	[ta'lerka]
saucer	сподак (м)	['spɔdak]
napkin (on table)	сурвэтка (ж)	[sur'vɛtka]
toothpick	зубачыстка (ж)	[zuba'tʃistka]

to order (meal)	заказаць	[zaka'zatsʲ]
course, dish	страва (ж)	['strava]
portion	порцыя (ж)	['pɔrtsiʲa]

appetizer	закуска (ж)	[za'kuska]
salad	салата (ж)	[sa'lata]
soup	суп (м)	['sup]

dessert	дэсерт (м)	[dɛ'sert]
jam (whole fruit jam)	варэнне (н)	[va'rɛnne]
ice-cream	марожанае (н)	[ma'roʒanae]

check	рахунак (м)	[ra'hunak]
to pay the check	аплаціць рахунак	[apla'tsitsʲ ra'hunak]
tip	чаявыя (мн)	[tʃaʲa'vʲia]

13. House. Apartment. Part 1

house	дом (м)	['dɔm]
country house	загарадны дом (м)	['zaɦaradnɨ 'dɔm]
villa (seaside ~)	віла (ж)	['vila]

floor, story	паверх (м)	[pa'verh]
entrance	пад'езд (м)	[pad"est]
wall	сцяна (ж)	[stsʲa'na]
roof	дах (м)	['dah]
chimney	комін (м)	['kɔmin]

attic (storage place)	гарышча (н)	[ɦa'riʃɕa]
window	акно (н)	[ak'nɔ]
window ledge	падаконнік (м)	[pada'kɔnnik]
balcony	балкон (м)	[bal'kɔn]

stairs (stairway)	лесвіца (ж)	['lesvitsa]
mailbox	паштовая скрынка (ж)	[paʃ'tɔvaʲa 'skrinka]
garbage can	бак (м) для смецця	[baɦ dlʲa 'smetsʲa]
elevator	ліфт (м)	['lift]

electricity	электрычнасць (ж)	[ɛlekt'ritʃnastsʲ]
light bulb	лямпачка (ж)	['lʲampatʃka]
switch	выключальнік (м)	[viklʉ'tʃalʲnik]
wall socket	разетка (ж)	[ra'zetka]
fuse	засцерагальнік (м)	[zasʲtsera'ɦalʲnik]

door	дзверы (мн)	[dzʲ'veri]
handle, doorknob	ручка (ж)	['rutʃka]
key	ключ (м)	['klʉtʃ]
doormat	дыванок (м)	[diva'nɔk]

door lock	замок (м)	[za'mɔk]
doorbell	званок (м)	[zva'nɔk]
knock (at the door)	стук (м)	['stuk]
to knock (vi)	стукаць	['stukatsʲ]
peephole	вочка (н)	['vɔtʃka]

yard	двор (м)	['dvɔr]
garden	сад (м)	['sat]
swimming pool	басейн (м)	[ba'sejn]
gym (home gym)	спартыўная зала (ж)	[spar'tiwnaʲa 'zala]
tennis court	тэнісны корт (м)	['tɛnisnɨ 'kɔrt]
garage	гараж (м)	[ɦa'raʃ]

private property	прыватная ўласнасць (ж)	[prɨ'vatnaʲa u'lasnasʲtʲsʲ]
warning sign	папераджальны надпіс (м)	[papera'ʤalʲnɨ 'natpis]
security	ахова (ж)	[a'hɔva]
security guard	ахоўнік (м)	[a'hɔwnik]

renovations	рамонт (м)	[ra'mɔnt]
to renovate (vt)	рабіць рамонт	[ra'bitsʲ ra'mɔnt]
to put in order	прыводзіць у парадак	[prɨ'vɔʣitsʲ u pa'radak]
to paint (~ a wall)	фарбаваць	[farba'vatsʲ]
wallpaper	шпалеры (ж мн)	[ʃpa'lerɨ]
to varnish (vt)	пакрываць лакам	[pakrɨ'vatsʲ 'lakam]

pipe	труба (ж)	[tru'ba]
tools	інструменты (м мн)	[instru'mentɨ]
basement	падвал (м)	[pad'val]
sewerage (system)	каналізацыя (ж)	[kanali'zatsɨʲa]

14. House. Apartment. Part 2

apartment	кватэра (ж)	[kva'tɛra]
room	пакой (м)	[pa'kɔj]
bedroom	спальня (ж)	['spalʲnʲa]
dining room	сталоўка (ж)	[sta'lɔwka]

living room	гасцёўня (ж)	[ɦas'tsʲɔwnʲa]
study (home office)	кабінет (м)	[kabi'net]
entry room	вітальня (ж)	[vi'talʲnʲa]
bathroom (room with a bath or shower)	ванны пакой (м)	['vannɨ pa'kɔj]
half bath	прыбіральня (ж)	[prɨbi'ralʲnʲa]

floor	падлога (ж)	[pad'lɔɦa]
ceiling	столь (ж)	['stɔlʲ]
to dust (vt)	выціраць пыл	[vɨtsi'ratsʲ 'pɨl]
vacuum cleaner	пыласос (м)	[pɨla'sɔs]
to vacuum (vt)	пыласосіць	[pɨla'sɔsitsʲ]

mop	швабра (ж)	['ʃvabra]
dust cloth	ануча (ж)	[a'nutʃa]
short broom	венік (м)	['venik]
dustpan	шуфлік (м) для смецця	['ʃuflik dlʲa 'smetsʲsʲa]

furniture	мэбля (ж)	['mɛblʲa]
table	стол (м)	['stɔl]
chair	крэсла (н)	['krɛsla]
armchair	фатэль (м)	[fa'tɛlʲ]

bookcase	шафа (ж)	['ʃafa]
shelf	паліца (ж)	[pa'liʦa]
wardrobe	шафа (ж)	['ʃafa]

mirror	люстэрка (н)	[lʉs'tɛrka]
carpet	дыван (м)	[dʲi'van]
fireplace	камін (м)	[ka'min]
drapes	шторы (мн)	['ʃtɔrʲi]
table lamp	настольная лямпа (ж)	[na'stɔlʲnaʲa 'lʲampa]
chandelier	люстра (ж)	['lʉstra]

kitchen	кухня (ж)	['kuhnʲa]
gas stove (range)	пліта (ж) газавая	[pli'ta 'hazavaʲa]
electric stove	пліта (ж) электрычная	[pli'ta ɛlɛkt'ritʃnaʲa]
microwave oven	мікрахвалевая печ (ж)	[mikra'hvalevaʲa 'petʃ]

refrigerator	халадзільнік (м)	[hala'dzilʲnik]
freezer	маразілка (ж)	[mara'zilka]
dishwasher	пасудамыечная машына (ж)	[pasuda'mʲetʃnaʲa ma'ʃina]
faucet	кран (м)	['kran]

meat grinder	мясарубка (ж)	[mʲasa'rupka]
juicer	сокавыціскалка (ж)	[sɔkavʲiʦi'skalka]
toaster	тостэр (м)	['tɔstɛr]
mixer	міксер (м)	['mikser]

coffee machine	кававарка (ж)	[kava'varka]
kettle	чайнік (м)	['tʃajnik]
teapot	імбрычак (м)	[im'britʃak]

TV set	тэлевізар (м)	[tɛle'vizar]
VCR (video recorder)	відэамагнітафон (м)	['vidɛa mahnita'fɔn]
iron (e.g., steam ~)	прас (м)	['pras]
telephone	тэлефон (м)	[tɛle'fɔn]

15. Professions. Social status

director	дырэктар (м)	[dʲi'rɛktar]
superior	начальнік (м)	[na'tʃalʲnik]
president	прэзідэнт (м)	[prɛzi'dɛnt]
assistant	памочнік (м)	[pa'mɔtʃnik]
secretary	сакратар (м)	[sakra'tar]
owner, proprietor	уладальнік (м)	[ula'dalʲnik]
partner	партнёр (м)	[part'nʲor]

stockholder	акцыянер (м)	[aktsiⁱa'ner]
businessman	бізнэсмен (м)	[biznɛs'men]
millionaire	мільянер (м)	[milⁱa'ner]
billionaire	мільярдэр (м)	[milⁱar'dɛr]

actor	акцёр (м)	[ak'tsⁱor]
architect	архітэктар (м)	[arhi'tɛktar]
banker	банкір (м)	[ban'kir]
broker	брокер (м)	['brɔker]

veterinarian	ветэрынар (м)	[vetɛri'nar]
doctor	урач (м)	[u'ratʃ]
chambermaid	пакаёўка (ж)	[paka'ⁱowka]
designer	дызайнер (м)	[diⁱzajner]
correspondent	карэспандэнт (м)	[karɛspan'dɛnt]
delivery man	кур'ер (м)	[kur"er]

electrician	электрык (м)	[ɛ'lektrik]
musician	музыка (м)	[mu'zïka]
babysitter	нянька (ж)	['nⁱanⁱka]
hairdresser	цырульнік (м)	[tsi'rulⁱnik]
herder, shepherd	пастух (м)	[pas'tuh]

singer (masc.)	спявак (м)	[spⁱa'vak]
translator	перакладчык (м)	[pera'klatʃïk]
writer	пісьменнік (м)	[pisⁱ'mennik]
carpenter	цясляр (м)	[tsⁱasⁱ'lⁱar]
cook	повар (м)	['pɔvar]

fireman	пажарны (м)	[pa'ʒarnï]
police officer	паліцэйскі (м)	[pali'tsɛjski]
mailman	паштальён (м)	[paʃta'lⁱon]
programmer	праграміст (м)	[prafira'mist]
salesman (store staff)	прадавец (м)	[prada'vets]

worker	рабочы (м)	[ra'bɔtʃï]
gardener	садоўнік (м)	[sa'dɔwnik]
plumber	сантэхнік (м)	[san'tɛhnik]
dentist	стаматолаг (м)	[stama'tɔlafi]
flight attendant (fem.)	сцюардэса (ж)	[sⁱtsᵘar'dɛsa]

| dancer (masc.) | танцор (м) | [tan'tsɔr] |
| bodyguard | целаахоўнік (м) | [tselaa'hɔwnik] |

| scientist | навуковец (м) | [navu'kɔvets] |
| schoolteacher | настаўнік (м) | [na'stawnik] |

farmer	фермер (м)	['fermer]
surgeon	хірург (м)	[hi'rurfi]
miner	шахцёр (м)	[ʃah'tsⁱor]
chef (kitchen chef)	шэф-повар (м)	[ʃɛf'pɔvar]
driver	шафёр (м)	[ʃa'fⁱor]

16. Sport

kind of sports	від (м) спорту	['vit 'sportu]
soccer	футбол (м)	[fud'bɔl]
hockey	хакей (м)	[ha'kej]
basketball	баскетбол (м)	[basked'bɔl]
baseball	бейсбол (м)	[bejz'bɔl]
volleyball	валейбол (м)	[valej'bɔl]
boxing	бокс (м)	['bɔks]
wrestling	барацьба (ж)	[baradzj'ba]
tennis	тэніс (м)	['tɛnis]
swimming	плаванне (н)	['plavanne]
chess	шахматы (мн)	['ʃahmatɨ]
running	бег (м)	['beɦ]
athletics	лёгкая атлетыка (ж)	['lʲɔɦkaʲa at'letɨka]
figure skating	фігурнае катанне (н)	[fi'ɦurnae ka'tanne]
cycling	веласпорт (м)	[vela'spɔrt]
billiards	більярд (м)	[bi'lʲjart]
bodybuilding	бодыбілдынг (м)	[bɔdɨ'bildɨnɦ]
golf	гольф (м)	['ɦɔlʲf]
scuba diving	дайвінг (м)	['dajvinɦ]
sailing	парусны спорт (м)	['parusnɨ 'spɔrt]
archery	стральба (ж) з лука	[stralʲ'ba z 'luka]
period, half	тайм (м)	['tajm]
half-time	перапынак (м)	[pera'pɨnak]
tie	нічыя (ж)	[nitʃɨ'ʲa]
to tie (vi)	згуляць унічыю	[zɦu'lʲatsʲ unitʃɨ'ʉ]
treadmill	бегавая дарожка (ж)	[beɦa'vaʲa da'rɔʃka]
player	гулец (м)	[ɦu'lets]
substitute	запасны гулец (м)	[zapas'nɨ ɦu'lets]
substitutes bench	лаўка (ж) запасных	['lawka zapas'nɨɦ]
match	матч (м)	['matʃ]
goal	вароты (мн)	[va'rɔtɨ]
goalkeeper	варатар (м)	[vara'tar]
goal (score)	гол (м)	['ɦɔl]
Olympic Games	Алімпійскія гульні (ж мн)	[alim'pijskiʲa 'ɦulʲni]
to set a record	ставіць рэкорд	['stavitsʲ rɛ'kɔrt]
final	фінал (м)	[fi'nal]
champion	чэмпіён (м)	[tʃɛmpi'ʲon]
championship	чэмпіянат (м)	[tʃɛmpiʲa'nat]
winner	пераможца (м)	[pera'mɔʃtsa]
victory	перамога (ж)	[pera'mɔɦa]
to win (vi)	выйграць	['vijɦratsʲ]

| to lose (not win) | прайграць | [praj'ɦratsʲ] |
| medal | медаль (м) | [me'dalʲ] |

first place	першае месца (н)	['perʃae 'mestsa]
second place	другое месца (н)	[dru'ɦɔe 'mestsa]
third place	трэцяе месца (н)	['trɛtsʲae 'mestsa]

stadium	стадыён (м)	[stadiʲon]
fan, supporter	заўзятар (м)	[zaw'zʲatar]
trainer, coach	трэнер (м)	['trɛner]
training	трэніроўка (ж)	[trɛni'rɔwka]

17. Foreign languages. Orthography

language	мова (ж)	['mɔva]
to study (vt)	вывучаць	[vivu'tʃatsʲ]
pronunciation	вымаўленне (н)	[vimaw'lenne]
accent	акцэнт (м)	[ak'tsɛnt]

noun	назоўнік (м)	[na'zɔwnik]
adjective	прыметнік (м)	[priˈmetnik]
verb	дзеяслоў (м)	[dzeʲa'slɔw]
adverb	прыслоўе (н)	[priˈslɔwe]

pronoun	займеннік (м)	[zaj'mennik]
interjection	выклічнік (м)	[vik'litʃnik]
preposition	прыназоўнік (м)	[prina'zɔwnik]

root	корань (м) слова	['kɔranʲ 'slɔva]
ending	канчатак (м)	[kan'tʃatak]
prefix	прыстаўка (ж)	[priˈstawka]
syllable	склад (м)	['sklat]
suffix	суфікс (м)	['sufiks]

stress mark	націск (м)	['natsisk]
period, dot	кропка (ж)	['krɔpka]
comma	коска (ж)	['kɔska]
colon	двукроп'е (н)	[dvu'krɔpʲe]
ellipsis	шматкроп'е (н)	[ʃmat'krɔpʲe]

question	пытанне (н)	[piˈtanne]
question mark	пытальнік (м)	[piˈtalʲnik]
exclamation point	клічнік (м)	['klitʃnik]

in quotation marks	у двукоссі	[u dvu'kɔssi]
in parenthesis	у дужках	[u 'duʃkah]
letter	літара (ж)	['litara]
capital letter	вялікая літара (ж)	[vʲa'likaʲa 'litara]
sentence	сказ (м)	['skas]
group of words	словазлучэнне (н)	[slɔvazlu'tʃɛnne]

expression	выраз (м)	['viras]
subject	дзейнік (м)	['dzejnik]
predicate	выказнік (м)	[vi'kazʲnik]
line	радок (м)	[ra'dɔk]
paragraph	абзац (м)	[ab'zaʦ]
synonym	сінонім (м)	[si'nɔnim]
antonym	антонім (м)	[an'tɔnim]
exception	выключэнне (н)	[viklʉ'tʃɛnne]
to underline (vt)	падкрэсліць	[pat'krɛslitsʲ]
rules	правілы (н мн)	['pravili]
grammar	граматыка (ж)	[ɦra'matika]
vocabulary	лексіка (ж)	['leksika]
phonetics	фанетыка (ж)	[fa'netika]
alphabet	алфавіт (м)	[alfa'vit]
textbook	падручнік (м)	[pad'rutʃnik]
dictionary	слоўнік (м)	['slɔwnik]
phrasebook	размоўнік (м)	[raz'mɔwnik]
word	слова (н)	['slɔva]
meaning	сэнс (м)	['sɛns]
memory	памяць (ж)	['pamʲatsʲ]

18. The Earth. Geography

the Earth	Зямля (ж)	[zʲam'lʲa]
the globe (the Earth)	зямны шар (м)	[zʲam'ni 'ʃar]
planet	планета (ж)	[pla'neta]
geography	геаграфія (ж)	[ɦea'ɦrafiʲa]
nature	прырода (ж)	[pri'rɔda]
map	карта (ж)	['karta]
atlas	атлас (м)	[at'las]
in the north	на поўначы	[na 'pɔwnatʃi]
in the south	на поўдні	[na 'pɔwdni]
in the west	на захадзе	[na 'zahadze]
in the east	на ўсходзе	[na w'shɔdze]
sea	мора (н)	['mɔra]
ocean	акіян (м)	[aki'ʲan]
gulf (bay)	заліў (м)	[za'liw]
straits	праліў (м)	[pra'liw]
continent (mainland)	мацярык (м)	[matsʲa'rik]
island	востраў (м)	['vɔstraw]
peninsula	паўвостраў (м)	[paw'vɔstraw]
archipelago	архіпелаг (м)	[arhipe'laɦ]

harbor	гавань (ж)	['ɦavanʲ]
coral reef	каралавы рыф (м)	[ka'ralavɨ 'rif]
shore	бераг (м)	['beraɦ]
coast	узбярэжжа (н)	[uzbʲa'rɛʐa]
flow (flood tide)	прыліў (м)	[prɨ'liw]
ebb (ebb tide)	адліў (м)	[ad'liw]
latitude	шырата (ж)	[ʃɨra'ta]
longitude	даўгата (ж)	[dawɦa'ta]
parallel	паралель (ж)	[para'lelʲ]
equator	экватар (м)	[ɛk'vatar]
sky	неба (н)	['neba]
horizon	гарызонт (м)	[ɦarɨ'zɔnt]
atmosphere	атмасфера (ж)	[atma'sfera]
mountain	гара (ж)	[ɦa'ra]
summit, top	вяршыня (ж)	[vʲar'ʃɨnʲa]
cliff	скала (ж)	[ska'la]
hill	узгорак (м)	[uz'ɦɔrak]
volcano	вулкан (м)	[vul'kan]
glacier	ледавік (м)	[leda'vik]
waterfall	вадаспад (м)	[vada'spat]
plain	раўніна (ж)	[raw'nina]
river	рака (ж)	[ra'ka]
spring (natural source)	крыніца (ж)	[krɨ'nitsa]
bank (of river)	бераг (м)	['beraɦ]
downstream (adv)	уніз па цячэнню	[u'nis pa tsʲa'tʃɛnnʉ]
upstream (adv)	уверх па цячэнню	[u'vɛrh pa tsʲa'tʃɛnnʉ]
lake	возера (н)	['vɔzera]
dam	плаціна (ж)	[pla'tsina]
canal	канал (м)	[ka'nal]
swamp (marshland)	балота (н)	[ba'lɔta]
ice	лёд (м)	['lʲot]

19. Countries of the world. Part 1

Europe	Еўропа	[ew'rɔpa]
European Union	Еўрапейскі саюз	[ewra'pejski sa'ʉs]
European (n)	еўрапеец (м)	[ewra'peets]
European (adj)	еўрапейскі	[ewra'pejski]
Austria	Аўстрыя	['awstrɨʲa]
Great Britain	Вялікабрытанія	[vʲalikabrɨ'taniʲa]
England	Англія	['anɦliʲa]
Belgium	Бельгія	['belʲɦiʲa]

Germany	Германія	[her'maniʲa]
Netherlands	Нідэрланды	[nidɛr'landɨ]
Holland	Галандыя	[ha'landʲa]
Greece	Грэцыя	['hrɛtsʲa]
Denmark	Данія	['daniʲa]
Ireland	Ірландыя	[ir'landʲa]

Iceland	Ісландыя	[is'landʲa]
Spain	Іспанія	[is'paniʲa]
Italy	Італія	[i'taliʲa]
Cyprus	Кіпр	['kipr]
Malta	Мальта	['malʲta]

Norway	Нарвегія	[nar'vehiʲa]
Portugal	Партугалія	[partu'haliʲa]
Finland	Фінляндыя	[fin'lʲandʲa]
France	Францыя	['frantsʲa]
Sweden	Швецыя	['ʃvetsʲa]

Switzerland	Швейцарыя	[ʃvej'tsarʲa]
Scotland	Шатландыя	[ʃat'landʲa]
Vatican	Ватыкан	[vatɨ'kan]
Liechtenstein	Ліхтэнштэйн	[lihtɛn'ʃtɛjn]
Luxembourg	Люксембург	[lʉksem'burh]

Monaco	Манака	[ma'naka]
Albania	Албанія	[al'baniʲa]
Bulgaria	Балгарыя	[bal'harʲa]

Hungary	Венгрыя	['venhrʲa]
Latvia	Латвія	['latviʲa]

Lithuania	Літва	[lit'va]
Poland	Польшча	['polʲʃɕa]
Romania	Румынія	[ru'mɨniʲa]

Serbia	Сербія	['serbiʲa]
Slovakia	Славакія	[sla'vakiʲa]

Croatia	Харватыя	[har'vatʲa]
Czech Republic	Чэхія	['tʃɛhiʲa]
Estonia	Эстонія	[ɛs'toniʲa]

Bosnia and Herzegovina	Боснія і Герцагавіна	['bosniʲa i hertsaha'vina]
Macedonia (Republic of ~)	Македонія	[make'doniʲa]

Slovenia	Славенія	[sla'veniʲa]
Montenegro	Чарнагорыя	[tʃarna'horʲa]
Belarus	Беларусь	[bela'rusʲ]
Moldova, Moldavia	Малдова	[mal'dova]
Russia	Расія	[ra'siʲa]
Ukraine	Украіна	[ukra'ina]

20. Countries of the world. Part 2

Asia	Азія	['aziᶦa]
Vietnam	В'етнам	[vʲet'nam]
India	Індыя	['indiᶦa]
Israel	Ізраіль	[iz'railʲ]
China	Кітай	[ki'taj]
Lebanon	Ліван	[li'van]
Mongolia	Манголія	[man'ɦoliᶦa]
Malaysia	Малайзія	[ma'lajziᶦa]
Pakistan	Пакістан	[paki'stan]
Saudi Arabia	Саудаўская Аравія	[sa'udawskaᶦa a'rawiᶦa]
Thailand	Тайланд	[taj'lant]
Taiwan	Тайвань	[taj'vanʲ]
Turkey	Турцыя	['turtsiᶦa]
Japan	Японія	[ᶦa'poniᶦa]
Afghanistan	Афганістан	[afɦani'stan]
Bangladesh	Бангладэш	[banɦla'dɛʃ]
Indonesia	Інданезія	[inda'neziᶦa]
Jordan	Іарданія	[iar'daniᶦa]
Iraq	Ірак	[i'rak]
Iran	Іран	[i'ran]
Cambodia	Камбоджа	[kam'bɔdʒa]
Kuwait	Кувейт	[ku'vejt]
Laos	Лаос	[la'ɔs]
Myanmar	М'янма	['mʲanma]
Nepal	Непал	[ne'pal]
United Arab Emirates	Аб'яднаныя Арабскія Эміраты	[abʲad'naniᶦa a'rapskiᶦa ɛmi'rati]
Syria	Сірыя	['siriᶦa]
Palestine	Палесцінская аўтаномія	[pales'tsinskaᶦa awta'nɔmiᶦa]
South Korea	Паўднёвая Карэя	[paw'dnʲovaᶦa ka'rɛᶦa]
North Korea	Паўночная Карэя	[paw'nɔtʃnaᶦa ka'rɛᶦa]
United States of America	Злучаныя Штаты Амерыкі	[zlutʃaniᶦa ʃtati a'meriki]
Canada	Канада	[ka'nada]
Mexico	Мексіка	['meksika]
Argentina	Аргенціна	[arɦen'tsina]
Brazil	Бразілія	[bra'ziliᶦa]
Colombia	Калумбія	[ka'lumbiᶦa]
Cuba	Куба	['kuba]
Chile	Чылі	['tʃili]
Venezuela	Венесуэла	[venesu'ɛla]

Ecuador	Эквадор	[ɛkvaˈdɔr]
The Bahamas	Багамскія астравы	[baˈɦamskiʲa astraˈvɨ]
Panama	Панама	[paˈnama]
Egypt	Егіпет	[eˈɦipet]
Morocco	Марока	[maˈrɔka]
Tunisia	Туніс	[tuˈnis]

Kenya	Кенія	[ˈkeniʲa]
Libya	Лівія	[ˈliviʲa]
South Africa	Паўднёва- Афрыканская Рэспубліка	[pawˈdnʲova afriˈkanskaʲa rɛsˈpublika]
Australia	Аўстралія	[awˈstraliʲa]
New Zealand	Новая Зеландыя	[ˈnovaʲa zeˈlandɨʲa]

21. Weather. Natural disasters

weather	надвор'е (н)	[naˈdvɔrʲe]
weather forecast	прагноз (м) надвор'я	[praɦˈnɔs nadˈvɔrʲʲa]
temperature	тэмпература (ж)	[tɛmperaˈtura]
thermometer	тэрмометр (м)	[tɛrˈmɔmetr]
barometer	барометр (м)	[baˈrɔmetr]

sun	сонца (н)	[ˈsɔntsa]
to shine (vi)	свяціць	[svʲaˈtsitsʲ]
sunny (day)	сонечны	[ˈsɔnetʃnɨ]
to come up (vi)	узысці	[uzɨsˈtsi]
to set (vi)	сесці	[ˈsesʲtsi]

rain	дождж (м)	[ˈdɔʃʤ]
it's raining	ідзе дождж	[iˈdze ˈdɔʃʤ]
pouring rain	праліўны дождж (м)	[praliwˈnɨ ˈdɔʃʤ]
rain cloud	хмара (ж)	[ˈhmara]
puddle	лужына (ж)	[ˈluʒɨna]
to get wet (in rain)	мокнуць	[ˈmɔknutsʲ]

thunderstorm	навальніца (ж)	[navalʲˈnitsa]
lightning (~ strike)	маланка (ж)	[maˈlanka]
to flash (vi)	бліскаць	[ˈbliskatsʲ]
thunder	гром (м)	[ˈɦrɔm]
it's thundering	грыміць гром	[ɦrɨˈmitsʲ ˈɦrɔm]
hail	град (м)	[ˈɦrat]
it's hailing	ідзе град	[iˈdze ˈɦrat]

heat (extreme ~)	гарачыня (ж)	[ɦaratʃɨˈnʲa]
it's hot	горача	[ˈɦɔratʃa]
it's warm	цёпла	[ˈtsʲopla]
it's cold	холадна	[ˈhɔladna]
fog (mist)	туман (м)	[tuˈman]
foggy	туманны	[tuˈmannɨ]

cloud	воблака (н)	['vɔblaka]
cloudy (adj)	воблачны	['vɔblatʃnɨ]
humidity	вільготнасць (ж)	[vilʲ'hɔtnastsʲ]

snow	снег (м)	['sneɦ]
it's snowing	ідзе снег	[i'dze 'sneɦ]
frost (severe ~, freezing cold)	мароз (м)	[ma'rɔs]
below zero (adv)	ніжэй за нуль	[ni'ʒɛj za 'nulʲ]
hoarfrost	шэрань (ж)	['ʃɛranʲ]

bad weather	непагадзь (ж)	['nepaɦatsʲ]
disaster	катастрофа (ж)	[kata'strɔfa]
flood, inundation	паводка (ж)	[pa'vɔtka]
avalanche	лавіна (ж)	[la'vina]
earthquake	землятрус (м)	[zemlʲa'trus]

tremor, quake	штуршок (м)	[ʃtur'ʃɔk]
epicenter	эпіцэнтр (м)	[ɛpi'tsɛntr]
eruption	вывяржэнне (н)	[vivʲar'ʒɛnne]
lava	лава (ж)	['lava]

tornado	тарнада (м)	[tar'nada]
twister	смерч (м)	['smertʃ]
hurricane	ураган (м)	[ura'ɦan]
tsunami	цунамі (н)	[tsu'nami]
cyclone	цыклон (м)	[tsɨk'lɔn]

22. Animals. Part 1

| animal | жывёліна (ж) | [ʒɨ'vʲolina] |
| predator | драпежнік (м) | [dra'peʒnik] |

tiger	тыгр (м)	['tiɦr]
lion	леў (м)	['lew]
wolf	воўк (м)	['vɔwk]
fox	ліса (ж)	['lisa]
jaguar	ягуар (м)	[ʲaɦu'ar]

lynx	рысь (ж)	['risʲ]
coyote	каёт (м)	[ka'ʲot]
jackal	шакал (м)	[ʃa'kal]
hyena	гіена (ж)	[ɦi'ena]

squirrel	вавёрка (ж)	[va'vʲorka]
hedgehog	вожык (м)	['vɔʒɨk]
rabbit	трус (м)	['trus]
raccoon	янот (м)	[ʲa'nɔt]
hamster	хамяк (м)	[ha'mʲak]
mole	крот (м)	['krɔt]

mouse	мыш (ж)	['miʃ]
rat	пацук (м)	[pa'ʦuk]
bat	кажан (м)	[ka'ʒan]

beaver	бабёр (м)	[ba'bʲor]
horse	конь (м)	['konʲ]
deer	алень (м)	[a'lenʲ]
camel	вярблюд (м)	[vʲar'blʉt]
zebra	зебра (ж)	['zebra]

whale	кіт (м)	['kit]
seal	цюлень (м)	[ʦʉ'lenʲ]
walrus	морж (м)	['morʃ]
dolphin	дэльфін (м)	[dɛlʲ'fin]

bear	мядзведзь (м)	[mʲadz'vedzʲ]
monkey	малпа (ж)	['malpa]
elephant	слон (м)	['slon]
rhinoceros	насарог (м)	[nasa'roɦ]
giraffe	жырафа (ж)	[ʒi'rafa]

hippopotamus	бегемот (м)	[beɦe'mot]
kangaroo	кенгуру (м)	[kenɦu'ru]
cat	кошка (ж)	['koʃka]
dog	сабака (м)	[sa'baka]

cow	карова (ж)	[ka'rova]
bull	бык (м)	['bik]
sheep (ewe)	авечка (ж)	[a'vetʃka]
goat	каза (ж)	[ka'za]

donkey	асёл (м)	[a'sʲol]
pig, hog	свіння (ж)	[svi'nnʲa]
hen (chicken)	курыца (ж)	['kuriʦa]
rooster	певень (м)	['pevenʲ]

duck	качка (ж)	['katʃka]
goose	гусь (ж)	['ɦusʲ]
turkey (hen)	індычка (ж)	[in'ditʃka]
sheepdog	аўчарка (ж)	[aw'tʃarka]

23. Animals. Part 2

bird	птушка (ж)	['ptuʃka]
pigeon	голуб (м)	['ɦolup]
sparrow	верабей (м)	[vera'bej]
tit (great tit)	сініца (ж)	[si'niʦa]
magpie	сарока (ж)	[sa'roka]
eagle	арол (м)	[a'rol]
hawk	ястраб (м)	['ʲastrap]

falcon	сокал (м)	['sɔkal]
swan	лебедзь (м)	['lebetsʲ]
crane	журавель (м)	[ʒura'velʲ]
stork	бусел (м)	['busel]
parrot	папугай (м)	[papu'ɦaj]
peacock	паўлін (м)	[paw'lin]
ostrich	страус (м)	['straus]

heron	чапля (ж)	['tʃaplʲa]
nightingale	салавей (м)	[sala'vej]
swallow	ластаўка (ж)	['lastawka]
woodpecker	дзяцел (м)	['dzʲatsel]
cuckoo	зязюля (ж)	[zʲa'zʉlʲa]
owl	сава (ж)	[sa'va]

penguin	пінгвін (м)	[pinɦ'vin]
tuna	тунец (м)	[tu'nets]
trout	стронга (ж)	['strɔnɦa]
eel	вугор (м)	[vu'ɦɔr]

shark	акула (ж)	[a'kula]
crab	краб (м)	['krap]
jellyfish	медуза (ж)	[me'duza]
octopus	васьміног (м)	[vasʲmi'nɔɦ]

starfish	марская зорка (ж)	[mar'skaʲa 'zɔrka]
sea urchin	марскі вожык (м)	[mar'ski 'vɔʒɨk]
seahorse	марскі конік (м)	[mar'ski 'kɔnik]
shrimp	крэветка (ж)	[krɛ'vetka]

snake	змяя (ж)	[zmæ'ʲa]
viper	гадзюка (ж)	[ɦa'dzʉka]
lizard	яшчарка (ж)	['ʲaʃɕarka]
iguana	ігуана (ж)	[iɦu'ana]

| chameleon | хамелеон (м) | [hamele'ɔn] |
| scorpion | скарпіён (м) | [skarpi'ʲon] |

turtle	чарапаха (ж)	[tʃara'paha]
frog	жаба (ж)	['ʒaba]
crocodile	кракадзіл (м)	[kraka'dzil]

| insect, bug | насякомае (н) | [nasʲa'kɔmae] |
| butterfly | матылёк (м) | [matɨ'lʲok] |

| ant | мурашка (ж) | [mu'raʃka] |
| fly | муха (ж) | ['muha] |

mosquito	камар (м)	[ka'mar]
beetle	жук (м)	['ʒuk]
bee	пчала (ж)	[ptʃa'la]
spider	павук (м)	[pa'vuk]

24. Trees. Plants

tree	дрэва (н)	['drɛva]
birch	бяроза (ж)	[bʲa'rɔza]
oak	дуб (м)	['dup]
linden tree	ліпа (ж)	['lipa]
aspen	асіна (ж)	[a'sina]

maple	клён (м)	['klʲon]
spruce	елка (ж)	['elka]
pine	сасна (ж)	[sas'na]
cedar	кедр (м)	['kedr]

poplar	таполя (ж)	[ta'pɔlʲa]
rowan	рабіна (ж)	[ra'bina]
beech	бук (м)	['buk]
elm	вяз (м)	['vʲas]

ash (tree)	ясень (м)	['ʲasenʲ]
chestnut	каштан (м)	[kaʃ'tan]
palm tree	пальма (ж)	['palʲma]
bush	куст (м)	['kust]

mushroom	грыб (м)	['ɦrip]
poisonous mushroom	атрутны грыб (м)	[a'trutnɨ 'ɦrip]
cep (Boletus edulis)	баравік (м)	[bara'vik]
russula	сыраежка (ж)	[sɨra'eʃka]
fly agaric	мухамор (м)	[muha'mɔr]
death cap	паганка (ж)	[pa'ɦanka]

flower	кветка (ж)	['kvetka]
bouquet (of flowers)	букет (м)	[bu'ket]
rose (flower)	ружа (ж)	['ruʒa]
tulip	цюльпан (м)	[tsʉlʲ'pan]
carnation	гваздзік (м)	[ɦvazʲ'dzik]

camomile	рамонак (м)	[ra'mɔnak]
cactus	кактус (м)	['kaktus]
lily of the valley	ландыш (м)	['landɨʃ]
snowdrop	падснежнік (м)	[pat'sneʒnik]
water lily	гарлачык (м)	[ɦar'latʃɨk]

greenhouse (tropical ~)	аранжарэя (ж)	[aranʒa'rɛʲa]
lawn	газон (м)	[ɦa'zɔn]
flowerbed	клумба (ж)	['klumba]

plant	расліна (ж)	[ras'lina]
grass	трава (ж)	[tra'va]
leaf	ліст (м)	['list]
petal	пялёстак (м)	[pʲa'lʲostak]
stem	сцябло (н)	[stsʲab'lɔ]

young plant (shoot)	расток (м)	[ras'tɔk]
cereal crops	зерневыя расліны (ж мн)	[zerneviͪa ra'slini]
wheat	пшаніца (ж)	[pʃa'nitsa]
rye	жыта (н)	['ʒita]
oats	авёс (м)	[a'vͪos]
millet	проса (н)	['prɔsa]
barley	ячмень (м)	[ͪatʃ'menͪ]
corn	кукуруза (ж)	[kuku'ruza]
rice	рыс (м)	['ris]

25. Various useful words

balance (of situation)	баланс (м)	[ba'lans]
base (basis)	база (ж)	['baza]
beginning	пачатак (м)	[pa'tʃatak]
category	катэгорыя (ж)	[katɛ'hɔriͪa]
choice	выбар (м)	['vibar]
coincidence	супадзенне (н)	[supa'dzenne]
comparison	параўнанне (н)	[paraw'nanne]
degree (extent, amount)	ступень (ж)	[stu'penͪ]
development	развіццё (н)	[razͪvi'tsͪo]
difference	адрозненне (н)	[ad'rɔzͪnenne]
effect (e.g., of drugs)	эфект (м)	[ɛ'fekt]
effort (exertion)	намаганне (н)	[nama'hanne]
element	элемент (м)	[ɛle'ment]
example (illustration)	прыклад (м)	['priklat]
fact	факт (м)	['fakt]
help	дапамога (ж)	[dapa'mɔha]
ideal	ідэал (м)	[idɛ'al]
kind (sort, type)	від (м)	['vit]
mistake, error	памылка (ж)	[pa'miɫka]
moment	момант (м)	['mɔmant]
obstacle	перашкода (ж)	[pera'ʃkɔda]
part (~ of sth)	частка (ж)	['tʃastka]
pause (break)	паўза (ж)	['pawza]
position	пазіцыя (ж)	[pa'zitsiͪa]
problem	праблема (ж)	[prab'lema]
process	працэс (м)	[pra'tsɛs]
progress	прагрэс (м)	[prah'rɛs]
property (quality)	уласцівасць (ж)	[ulas'tsivastsͪ]
reaction	рэакцыя (ж)	[rɛ'aktsiͪa]
risk	рызыка (ж)	['rizika]

| secret | таямніца (ж) | [taˡam'niʦa] |
| series | серыя (ж) | ['seriʲa] |

shape (outer form)	форма (ж)	['fɔrma]
situation	сітуацыя (ж)	[situ'aʦiʲa]
solution	рашэнне (н)	[ra'ʃɛnne]
standard (adj)	стандартны	[stan'dartnɨ]

stop (pause)	перапынак (м)	[pera'pɨnak]
style	стыль (м)	['stilʲ]
system	сістэма (ж)	[sis'tɛma]
table (chart)	табліца (ж)	[tab'liʦa]
tempo, rate	тэмп (м)	['tɛmp]

term (word, expression)	тэрмін (м)	['tɛrmin]
truth (e.g., moment of ~)	ісціна (ж)	['isˡʦina]
turn (please wait your ~)	чарга (ж)	[ʧar'ha]
urgent (adj)	тэрміновы	[tɛrmi'nɔvɨ]

utility (usefulness)	карысць (ж)	[ka'risʦʲ]
variant (alternative)	варыянт (м)	[variˡʲant]
way (means, method)	спосаб (м)	['spɔsap]
zone	зона (ж)	['zɔna]

26. Modifiers. Adjectives. Part 1

additional (adj)	дадатковы	[dadat'kɔvɨ]
ancient (~ civilization)	старажытны	[stara'ʒɨtnɨ]
artificial (adj)	штучны	['ʃtuʧnɨ]
bad (adj)	дрэнны	['drɛnnɨ]
beautiful (person)	прыгожы	[pri'hɔʒɨ]

big (in size)	вялікі	[vʲa'liki]
bitter (taste)	горкі	['hɔrki]
blind (sightless)	сляпы	[sʲlʲa'pɨ]
central (adj)	цэнтральны	[ʦɛn'tralʲnɨ]

children's (adj)	дзіцячы	[dʑi'ʦˡʲaʧʲi]
clandestine (secret)	падпольны	[pat'polʲnɨ]
clean (free from dirt)	чысты	['ʧɨsti]
clever (smart)	разумны	[ra'zumnɨ]
compatible (adj)	сумяшчальны	[sumʲa'ʃʧalʲnɨ]

contented (satisfied)	задаволены	[zada'vɔlenɨ]
dangerous (adj)	небяспечны	[nebʲas'peʧnɨ]
dead (not alive)	мёртвы	['mʲortvɨ]
dense (fog, smoke)	густы	[hus'tɨ]
difficult (decision)	цяжкі	['ʦˡʲaʃki]
dirty (not clean)	брудны	['brudnɨ]
easy (not difficult)	лёгкі	['lʲohki]

empty (glass, room)	пусты	[pusˈtɨ]
exact (amount)	дакладны	[daˈkladnɨ]
excellent (adj)	выдатны	[vɨˈdatnɨ]

excessive (adj)	празмерны	[prazˈmernɨ]
exterior (adj)	вонкавы	[ˈvɔnkavɨ]
fast (quick)	хуткі	[ˈhutki]
fertile (land, soil)	урадлівы	[uradˈlivɨ]
fragile (china, glass)	ломкі	[ˈlɔmki]

free (at no cost)	бясплатны	[bʲasˈplatnɨ]
fresh (~ water)	прэсны	[ˈprɛsnɨ]
frozen (food)	замарожаны	[zamaˈrɔʒanɨ]
full (completely filled)	поўны	[ˈpɔwnɨ]
happy (adj)	шчаслівы	[ʃɕasˈlivɨ]

hard (not soft)	цвёрды	[ˈtsvʲordɨ]
huge (adj)	вялізны	[vʲaˈliznɨ]
ill (sick, unwell)	хворы	[ˈhvɔrɨ]
immobile (adj)	нерухомы	[neruˈhɔmɨ]
important (adj)	важны	[ˈvaʒnɨ]

interior (adj)	унутраны	[uˈnutranɨ]
last (e.g., ~ week)	мінулы	[miˈnulɨ]
last (final)	апошні	[aˈpɔʃni]
left (e.g., ~ side)	левы	[ˈlevɨ]
legal (legitimate)	законны	[zaˈkɔnnɨ]

light (in weight)	лёгкі	[ˈlʲofiki]
liquid (fluid)	вадкі	[ˈvatki]
long (e.g., ~ hair)	доўгі	[ˈdɔwfii]
loud (voice, etc.)	гучны	[ˈhutʃnɨ]
low (voice)	ціхі	[ˈtsihi]

27. Modifiers. Adjectives. Part 2

main (principal)	галоўны	[ɦaˈlɔwnɨ]
matt, matte	матавы	[ˈmatavɨ]
mysterious (adj)	загадкавы	[zaˈɦatkavɨ]
narrow (street, etc.)	вузкі	[ˈvuski]
native (~ country)	родны	[ˈrɔdnɨ]

negative (~ response)	адмоўны	[adˈmɔwnɨ]
new (adj)	новы	[ˈnɔvɨ]
next (e.g., ~ week)	наступны	[naˈstupnɨ]
normal (adj)	нармальны	[narˈmalʲni]
not difficult (adj)	няцяжкі	[nʲaˈtsʲaʃki]

| obligatory (adj) | абавязковы | [abavʲasˈkɔvɨ] |
| old (house) | стары | [staˈri] |

open (adj)	адчынены	[a'tʃineni]
opposite (adj)	супрацьлеглы	[supratsʲ'leɦli]
ordinary (usual)	звычайны	[zvi'tʃajni]

original (unusual)	арыгінальны	[ariɦi'nalʲni]
personal (adj)	асабісты	[asa'bisti]
polite (adj)	ветлівы	['vetlivi]
poor (not rich)	бедны	['bedni]
possible (adj)	магчымы	[maɦ'tʃimi]
principal (main)	асноўны	[as'nɔwni]
probable (adj)	імаверны	[ima'verni]
prolonged (e.g., ~ applause)	працяглы	[pra'tsʲaɦli]
public (open to all)	грамадскі	[ɦra'matski]

rare (adj)	рэдкі	['rɛtki]
raw (uncooked)	сыры	[si'ri]
right (not left)	правы	['pravi]
ripe (fruit)	спелы	['speli]

risky (adj)	рызыкоўны	[rizi'kɔwni]
sad (~ look)	сумны	['sumni]
second hand (adj)	ужываны	[uʒi'vani]
shallow (water)	мелкі	['melki]
sharp (blade, etc.)	востры	['vɔstri]
short (in length)	кароткі	[ka'rɔtki]
similar (adj)	падобны	[pa'dɔbni]
small (in size)	маленькі, малы	[ma'lenʲki], [ma'li]
smooth (surface)	гладкі	['ɦlatki]
soft (~ toys)	мяккі	['mʲakki]

solid (~ wall)	трывалы	[tri'vali]
sour (flavor, taste)	кіслы	['kisli]
spacious (house, etc.)	прасторны	[pra'stɔrni]
special (adj)	спецыяльны	[spetsi'alʲni]

straight (line, road)	прамы	[pra'mi]
strong (person)	моцны	['mɔtsni]
stupid (foolish)	дурны	[dur'ni]
superb, perfect (adj)	надзвычайны	[nadzvi'tʃajni]

sweet (sugary)	салодкі	[sa'lɔtki]
tan (adj)	загарэлы	[zaɦa'rɛli]
tasty (delicious)	смачны	['smatʃni]
unclear (adj)	незразумелы	[nezrazu'meli]

28. Verbs. Part 1

| to accuse (vt) | абвінавачваць | [abvina'vatʃvatsʲ] |
| to agree (say yes) | згаджацца | [zɦa'dʒatsa] |

to announce (vt)	абвяшчаць	[abvʲaˈʃɕatsʲ]
to answer (vi, vt)	адказваць	[atˈkazvatsʲ]
to apologize (vi)	прасіць прабачэння	[praˈsitsʲ prabaˈtʃɛnnʲa]

to arrive (vi)	прыязджаць	[prʲiˈaʒˈdʒatsʲ]
to ask (~ oneself)	пытаць	[pɨˈtatsʲ]
to be absent	адсутнічаць	[aˈtsutnitʃatsʲ]
to be afraid	баяцца	[baˈʲatsa]
to be born	нарадзіцца	[naraˈdzitsa]

to be in a hurry	спяшацца	[spʲaˈʃatsa]
to beat (to hit)	біць	[ˈbitsʲ]
to begin (vt)	пачынаць	[patʃiˈnatsʲ]
to believe (in God)	верыць	[ˈveritsʲ]
to belong to …	належаць	[naˈleʒatsʲ]
to break (split into pieces)	ламаць	[laˈmatsʲ]

to build (vt)	будаваць	[budaˈvatsʲ]
to buy (purchase)	купляць	[kupˈlʲatsʲ]
can (v aux)	магчы	[mahˈtʃi]
can (v aux)	магчы	[mahˈtʃi]
to cancel (call off)	скасаваць	[skasaˈvatsʲ]

to catch (vt)	лавіць	[laˈvitsʲ]
to change (vt)	змяніць	[zmʲaˈnitsʲ]
to check (to examine)	правяраць	[pravʲaˈratsʲ]
to choose (select)	выбіраць	[vɨbiˈratsʲ]
to clean up (tidy)	прыбіраць	[prʲibiˈratsʲ]

to close (vt)	зачыняць	[zatʃiˈnʲatsʲ]
to compare (vt)	параўноўваць	[parawˈnowvatsʲ]
to complain (vi, vt)	скардзіцца	[ˈskardzitsa]
to confirm (vt)	пацвердзіць	[patsˈverdzitsʲ]
to congratulate (vt)	віншаваць	[vinʃaˈvatsʲ]

to cook (dinner)	гатаваць	[hataˈvatsʲ]
to copy (vt)	скапіраваць	[skaˈpiravatsʲ]
to cost (vt)	каштаваць	[kaʃtaˈvatsʲ]
to count (add up)	лічыць	[liˈtʃitsʲ]
to count on …	разлічваць на …	[razˈlitʃvatsʲ na …]

to create (vt)	стварыць	[stvaˈritsʲ]
to cry (weep)	плакаць	[ˈplakatsʲ]
to dance (vi, vt)	танцаваць	[tantsaˈvatsʲ]
to deceive (vi, vt)	падманваць	[padˈmanvatsʲ]
to decide (~ to do sth)	вырашаць	[vɨraˈʃatsʲ]

to delete (vt)	выдаліць	[ˈvɨdalitsʲ]
to demand (request firmly)	патрабаваць	[patrabaˈvatsʲ]
to deny (vt)	адмаўляць	[admawˈlʲatsʲ]
to depend on …	залежаць ад …	[zaˈleʒatsʲ at …]
to despise (vt)	пагарджаць	[paharˈdʒatsʲ]

to die (vi)	памерці	[pa'mertsi]
to dig (vt)	капаць	[ka'patsʲ]
to disappear (vi)	прапасці	[pra'pasʲtsi]
to discuss (vt)	абмяркоўваць	[abmʲar'kowvatsʲ]
to disturb (vt)	турбаваць	[turba'vatsʲ]

29. Verbs. Part 2

to dive (vi)	нырaць	[nɨ'ratsʲ]
to divorce (vi)	развесціся	[raz'vesʲtsisʲa]
to do (vt)	рабіць	[ra'bitsʲ]
to doubt (have doubts)	сумнявацца	[sumnʲa'vatsa]
to drink (vi, vt)	піць	['pitsʲ]

to drop (let fall)	упускаць	[upus'katsʲ]
to dry (clothes, hair)	сушыць	[su'ʃɨtsʲ]
to eat (vi, vt)	есці	['esʲtsi]
to end (~ a relationship)	спыняць	[spɨ'nʲatsʲ]
to excuse (forgive)	прабачаць	[praba'ʧatsʲ]

to exist (vi)	існаваць	[isna'vatsʲ]
to expect (foresee)	прадбачыць	[prad'baʧɨtsʲ]
to explain (vt)	тлумачыць	[tlu'maʧɨtsʲ]
to fall (vi)	падаць	['padatsʲ]
to fight (street fight, etc.)	біцца	['bitsa]
to find (vt)	знаходзіць	[zna'hɔdzitsʲ]

to finish (vt)	заканчваць	[za'kanʧvatsʲ]
to fly (vi)	ляцець	[lʲa'tsetsʲ]
to forbid (vt)	забараніць	[zabara'nitsʲ]
to forget (vi, vt)	забываць	[zabɨ'vatsʲ]
to forgive (vt)	выбачаць	[vɨba'ʧatsʲ]

to get tired	стамляцца	[stam'lʲatsa]
to give (vt)	даваць	[da'vatsʲ]
to go (on foot)	ісці	[is'tsi]
to hate (vt)	ненавідзець	[nena'vidzetsʲ]

to have (vt)	мець	['metsʲ]
to have breakfast	снедаць	['snedatsʲ]
to have dinner	вячэраць	[vʲa'ʧɛratsʲ]
to have lunch	абедаць	[a'bedatsʲ]

to hear (vt)	чуць	['ʧutsʲ]
to help (vt)	дапамагаць	[dapama'hatsʲ]
to hide (vt)	хаваць	[ha'vatsʲ]
to hope (vi, vt)	спадзявацца	[spadzʲa'vatsa]
to hunt (vi, vt)	паляваць	[palʲa'vatsʲ]
to hurry (vi)	спяшацца	[spʲa'ʃatsa]
to insist (vi, vt)	настойваць	[na'stɔjvatsʲ]

to insult (vt)	абражаць	[abraˈʒatsʲ]
to invite (vt)	запрашаць	[zapraˈʃatsʲ]
to joke (vi)	жартаваць	[ʒartaˈvatsʲ]
to keep (vt)	захоўваць	[zaˈhɔwvatsʲ]

to kill (vt)	забіваць	[zabiˈvatsʲ]
to know (sb)	ведаць	[ˈvedatsʲ]
to know (sth)	ведаць	[ˈvedatsʲ]
to like (I like …)	падабацца	[padaˈbatsa]
to look at …	глядзець на …	[hlʲaˈdzetsʲ na …]

to lose (umbrella, etc.)	губляць	[hubˈlʲatsʲ]
to love (sb)	кахаць	[kaˈhatsʲ]
to make a mistake	памыляцца	[pamɨˈlʲatsa]
to meet (vi, vt)	сустракацца	[sustraˈkatsa]
to miss (school, etc.)	прапускаць	[prapusˈkatsʲ]

30. Verbs. Part 3

to obey (vi, vt)	падпарадкавацца	[patparatkaˈvatsa]
to open (vt)	адчыняць	[atʃɨˈnʲatsʲ]
to participate (vi)	удзельнічаць	[uˈdzelʲnitʃatsʲ]
to pay (vi, vt)	плаціць	[plaˈtsitsʲ]
to permit (vt)	дазваляць	[dazvaˈlʲatsʲ]

to play (children)	гуляць	[huˈlʲatsʲ]
to pray (vi, vt)	маліцца	[maˈlitsa]
to promise (vt)	абяцаць	[abʲaˈtsatsʲ]
to propose (vt)	прапаноўваць	[prapaˈnɔwvatsʲ]
to prove (vt)	даказваць	[daˈkazvatsʲ]
to read (vi, vt)	чытаць	[tʃɨˈtatsʲ]

to receive (vt)	атрымаць	[atrɨˈmatsʲ]
to rent (sth from sb)	наймаць	[najˈmatsʲ]
to repeat (say again)	паўтараць	[pawtaˈratsʲ]
to reserve, to book	рэзерваваць	[rɛzervaˈvatsʲ]
to run (vi)	бегчы	[ˈbehtʃi]

to save (rescue)	ратаваць	[rataˈvatsʲ]
to say (~ thank you)	сказаць	[skaˈzatsʲ]
to see (vt)	бачыць	[ˈbatʃitsʲ]
to sell (vt)	прадаваць	[pradaˈvatsʲ]
to send (vt)	адпраўляць	[atprawˈlʲatsʲ]
to shoot (vi)	страляць	[straˈlʲatsʲ]

to shout (vi)	крычаць	[krɨˈtʃatsʲ]
to show (vt)	паказваць	[paˈkazvatsʲ]
to sign (document)	падпісваць	[patˈpisvatsʲ]
to sing (vi)	пець	[ˈpetsʲ]
to sit down (vi)	садзіцца	[saˈdzitsa]

to smile (vi)	усміхацца	[usmi'hatsa]
to speak (vi, vt)	гаварыць	[ɦava'ritsʲ]
to steal (money, etc.)	красці	['krasʲtsi]
to stop (please ~ calling me)	спыняць	[spɨ'nʲatsʲ]
to study (vt)	вывучаць	[vɨvu'tʃatsʲ]
to swim (vi)	плаваць	['plavatsʲ]
to take (vt)	браць	['bratsʲ]
to talk to …	гаварыць з …	[ɦava'ritsʲ s …]
to tell (story, joke)	апавядаць	[apavʲa'datsʲ]
to thank (vt)	дзякаваць	['dzʲakavatsʲ]
to think (vi, vt)	думаць	['dumatsʲ]
to translate (vt)	перакладаць	[perakla'datsʲ]
to trust (vt)	давяраць	[davʲa'ratsʲ]
to try (attempt)	спрабаваць	[spraba'vatsʲ]
to turn (e.g., ~ left)	паварочваць	[pava'rotʃvatsʲ]
to turn off	выключаць	[vɨklʉ'tʃatsʲ]
to turn on	уключаць	[uklʉ'tʃatsʲ]
to understand (vt)	разумець	[razu'metsʲ]
to wait (vt)	чакаць	[tʃa'katsʲ]
to want (wish, desire)	хацець	[ha'tsetsʲ]
to work (vi)	працаваць	[pratsa'vatsʲ]
to write (vt)	пісаць	[pi'satsʲ]

www.ingramcontent.com/pod-product-compliance
Lightning Source LLC
Chambersburg PA
CBHW060029050426
42448CB00012B/2913

T&P Books Publishing

GUIDE DE CONVERSATION
— PERSAN —

LES PHRASES LES PLUS UTILES

Ce guide de conversation
contient les phrases et
les questions les plus
communes et nécessaires
pour communiquer avec
des étrangers

Par Andrey Taranov

T&P BOOKS

Guide de conversation + dictionnaire de 1500 mots

Guide de conversation Français-Persan et dictionnaire concis de 1500 mots

Par Andrey Taranov

La collection de guides de conversation "Tout ira bien!", publiée par T&P Books, est conçue pour les gens qui voyagent par affaire ou par plaisir. Les guides contiennent l'essentiel pour la communication de base. Il s'agit d'une série indispensable de phrases pour "survivre" à l'étranger.

Une autre section du livre contient un petit dictionnaire de plus de 1500 mots les plus utilisés. Le dictionnaire inclut beaucoup de termes gastronomiques et peut être utile lorsque vous faites le marché ou commandez des plats au restaurant.

T&P Books Publishing
www.tpbooks.com

ISBN: 978-1-78716-944-9

Ce livre existe également en format électronique.
Pour plus d'informations, veuillez consulter notre site: www.tpbooks.com
ou rendez-vous sur ceux des grandes librairies en ligne.